DISCLAIMER: No Masonic Secrets are revealed in the meditations found within these pages. The following are for contemplative and reasoning purposes only. Both Masons and non-Masons are invited to read and reflect.

Masonic Meditations
Vol. 2

Philosophy

Edited and Compiled by

RaMen

Authored by Dr. Jeff Menzise, 32°

Masonic Meditations Vol 2 - Philosophy

Copyright ©2019 by Jeff Menzise. All rights reserved. Printed in the United States of America. No part of this book may be used or reproduced in any manner without written permission from the author except in the case of brief quotations embodied in critical articles and reviews. For information address Mind on the Matter Publishing, Post Office Box 755, College Park, Maryland 20741.

10 9 8 7 6 5 4 3 2 1

Cover Artwork & Design by Jeffery Menzise, Ph.D. for Mind on the Matter Publishing

Library of Congress Cataloging-in-Publication Data
Menzise, Jeffery,
    Masonic Meditations Vol 2 - Philosophy/ by Jeff Menzise, Ph.D.
includes Foreword, Cover Artwork, & Design

ISBN 978-0-578-54388-8

Published in 2019 by
Mind on the Matter Publishing,
PO BOX 755, College Park, MD 20741
Website: www.mindonthematter.com
Email: drjeff@mindonthematter.com
Instagram & Twitter: @drjeffmenzise
Office Phone: 240-988-9639

Dedication

This book is dedicated to those truth seekers who journey through life seeking the answers to the questions that puzzle us all. I hope this series provides you with inspiration, insight, a thought-provoking exchange, and perhaps, answers.

Acknowledgment

We would like to thank the Phylaxis Society, the Phylaxis Magazine, Lux e Tenebris, as well as the Masonic Digest (published out of the Most Worshipful Prince Hall Grand Lodge of the District of Columbia) for originally publishing many of my thoughts shared in this series. We would also like to thank those who have requested a collection of Masonic writings authored by Dr. Jeff Menzise. We hope this response is sufficient.

Preface

This series presents an introductory view of my thoughts as both an initiate of several African spiritual systems, and an initiate up to the 32nd degree of the Scottish Rite and 10th degree of the York Rite, Prince Hall Freemasonry. The purpose for writing and now compiling this series is simply to offer an opinion and perspective on matters related to Freemasonry. The views that I provide are original but not necessarily unique, meaning, you may find similar statements shared by other Masonic and non-Masonic philosophers, authors, and scholars. The originality is in how I express these thoughts from my unique perspective having studied various philosophical systems, including the science of clinical psychology.

This three volume series is divided into the following subjects: Symbolism, Philosophy, and The Work. As a symbolist, I often seek the deeper meaning of both form and function; this is the theme running through volume one. Because Freemasonry is largely based on the symbolic form of communication, it has served as a field rich in resources for me to interpret and translate. The main feature of volume two, on philosophy, is a deep-dive into my views on the origins of Freemasonry as a system of human development. Finally, in volume three, I explore how the science of meditation and self-reflection is beneficial to Freemasons, within the context of our Craft.

There is something for everyone in this series. The wisdom and insights offered are universal and easily adapted to any existing religious and philosophical system or orientation. The practical tools offered alongside the cognitive exercise of reading each of the articles, is enough to form a new perspective for those who choose to engage the text on a deeper level.

Contents & Articles

Dedication v

Acknowledgment v

Preface... vii

True of Deed, True of Word 11

Thoughts on Mystery Systems
and Freemasonry.. 19

An African Rite Considered........................ 41

The Masonic Mind Defined 97

Freemasonry and the
African Influence 111

True of Deed, True of Word

By Jeff Menzise, Ph.D., 32°, FPS

*T*his thing called Truth. Many believe it to be totally personal and totally subjective, meaning everyone has their own version of the Truth based on his or her specific perspective. We've all heard the story of the four hoodwinked individuals trying to identify an elephant without the sense of sight. Each of the four had their hands on a particular part of the elephant, which gave them a uniquely limited and isolated perspective of the elephant. When the first man, standing by the leg, was asked what he was touching, he assuredly replied "a tree's trunk." When the woman standing by the elephant's ears was asked, she spoke with confidence in saying, "why, this is some sort of fan." The young boy up by the trunk was a bit puzzled, but with out a stutter clearly professed that he must be "handling a snake, an odd form, but a snake nonetheless." Lastly, the girl by the tail claimed the tail was simply a vine blowing in the wind.

This story (or some variation of it) has been used to demonstrate how perspectives can make sense based on the information given, but that they are also likely to fall short of reality. Perhaps the most troubling aspect of this story is the fact that these four hoodwinked individuals may never discover the truth about what they are observing. If left with their own line of reasoning long enough, they may grow in conviction regarding their conclusions and may also become more confident in their way of thinking. This is why people with a faulty logic, misinformation or an unrealistic reasoning scheme, are likely to consistently be incorrect about things. Stated another way, if my square is not at 90 degrees, but instead opens at 60, and I am unaware and still engage and use it as if it were at a right angle, I am destined to make mistakes. And just like our hoodwinked friends, I too may grow confident in my irregular tool, and may develop a certain conviction about my conclusions, and yes, may also be far from correct and thus, far from reality.

The above illustration is designed to show us how important it is to have proper tools for the job, but also the correct knowledge of how to use them. The truth is such a tool, and we have long figured out how to properly use it. But who's to say whose standard for measuring the truth is true? At this point in the discussion we need an open mind because, when something challenges our understanding of the truth, we can get defensive and closed. For the sake of this article, let's define the word truth as "that which is." A very simple concept stating that everything that "is" is "true;" and every thing that "is not" is not true. Take a deep breath and reread that sentence...not a play on words here. The high science of truth is the basic underlying principle that says ALL THINGS that are here, at some moment of time or another, are true.

For example, if it rained yesterday in Oklahoma City, then it is true that it rained in Oklahoma City yesterday, while you were in Tampa with clear skies. Is it true that because it didn't rain where you were that your truth is different than the person in Oklahoma City? No. Your experience was, but the truth is the same. What is, is, regardless of who knows, experiences, acknowledges, denies, or embraces it. Again this isn't a play on words beloved Sistars and Brothers, but an exercise designed to refine our mental processes, increase our reasoning abilities, and increase the likelihood that we will be True observers of reality, shining our Lights for all to see.

What are we if not Seekers of Light? What is Light if not Truth? For those of us on the Square, we are Seekers of That Which Is. We are in pursuit of the knowledge of creation; in other words, we are seeking to know how to make truth, to actually create that which is.

Let's return to the question of whose standard we shall use in order to discern truth from non-truth. In my opinion, your own self-made standard, which is as personal as the truth will ever get, is the best standard for measurement. By each individual using their own measure of the truth, while consciously realizing that their perspective is likely incorrect, they will give rise to opportunities to analyze and correct (if need be) their perspectives and how they view reality. So how do we measure the truth? Each of us knows the truth about what we do on a daily basis. Each of us knows where we were yesterday, where we are headed after work, who we saw, who we talked too, etc. Each of these directly knowable things are all gold standards when it comes to measuring the truth because we were present and know them to be reality (now during my clinical training, I experienced special cases where people were suffering from delusions and hallucinations, and thus, were incapable of discerning reality from fantasy).

Our Ancestors practiced an exercise designed to strengthen our ability to discern the truth, by actually using what we KNOW to be true, to gauge the validity of all other things. The idea was to get so acclimated to experiencing the truth by consciously living, representing and speaking the truth at every possible moment. Sounds easy right? It is easy; as easy as making a choice in the moment. So why is it that people lie so much? Why do we say things are, that are not? Why do we say things that are not, are? Fear. Plain and simple, it's the fear associated with our need to be accepted, our need to be respected, our need to be connected, and the fear of loss/punishment.

  Think about the husband that sneaks and drinks alcohol knowing that his wife disapproves. When he is confronted and asked if he has been consuming alcohol, he has to consider the consequences of telling the truth. Depending on the temperament of the husband, the wife, and the situation, he may end up divorced, in the "doghouse," on the couch, or in an argument that will not end well. Facing all of these potentially negative outcomes, it's understandable why an individual would decide to conceal that which is. However, the alternative (telling the truth) carries with it a subtle seed of power that, if properly harnessed, can lead to an overflowing of gifts and abilities derived directly from our individual will and creative centers.

True of Deed, True of Word

Once you have experienced what it consciously feels like to tell the truth, in the face of potential loss, potential harm, and fear, you will also, by default, get a clearer understanding of how those "un-truths" feel, and thus, will have increased your ability to discern true from false. The overarching purpose is to: 1) observe and analyze your own fear-based thoughts, speech, and/or actions; 2) understand the motivation for the fear; and 3) make the necessary changes to eliminate the fear and shame associated with the choices we make in life.

My Brothers and Sistars, once a person commits to living and representing the truth at every possible opportunity, they will eventually refine their lives in such a way that telling the truth no longer carries the risk of loss, injury, or shame as it once did. We eventually get to a point where we no longer have anything about our selves to hide in the shadows of the intentionally blocked Light. Our Ancestors called this state Maakheru. It is a position of power, of an autonomous and truly sovereign being, fully capable of creating their own reality by being the truth. This all ties directly into the

Divine utterance: "I am that I am."

    My advice is to start small, representing the truth on those things whose consequences are not so great in regards to the potential for loss. For example, a common lie often told by people is in response to someone asking about their well-being. Think about it, when someone asks "how are you?" we typically respond with "I'm good" even if we are feeling horrible, or "I can't complain" knowing that you actually can complain. To consciously modify this "knee-jerk" response pattern will assist our degree of awareness, which translates directly into our ability to catch negative behaviors before they happen and preventing a lie from ever "needing" to be told.

    Remember to always operate within the circumference of your circle and keep the angles sharp on your square. Do things within proper measure, even exercises such as this, which are designed to improve and refine our individual Lights.

THOUGHTS ON MYSTERY SYSTEMS AND FREEMASONRY

Jeff Menzise, Ph.D., 32°, FPS

The editor of The Phylaxis Magazine, Alton G. Roundtree, interviewed Brother Jeff Menzise, Ph.D. Brother Menzise has had extensive experience with Mystery Schools, and initiations. A biographical sketch of Brother Menzise follows:

Brother Jeff Menzise is a member of St. Johns Lodge No. 3, Prince White Chapter No. 1, HRAM, King Solomon Consistory No. 20, and is a member of the Prince Hall Council of Royal and Select Masters, all in Cincinnati, Ohio. He is a doctor of clinical psychology and is one of the foremost experts on mindfulness and various other psycho-spiritual modalities of prevention and therapeutic intervention. He is well known for his successful work with children, families, couples and adult individuals along various paths of life circumstances. He conducts training and workshops internationally for governments, cor-

porations, universities, primary and secondary schools, organizations and private groups. Dr. Menzise has taught in the Psychology and African Studies departments of various universities and is currently working as an Associate Professor with Morgan State University's Institute for Urban Research. He has published five books. His first book: Dumbing Down; Reflections on the Mis-education of the Negro was published in 2012; and his most recent book: Symbolically Speaking, Volume I, African Lodge No. 1, The Context was published in 2015. He also recently edited the Phylaxis Society book: The Greatest Prince Hall Mason of the 20th Century. Dr. Menzise was voted an "Actual Fellow" with the Phylaxis Society, and has published several articles in The Phylaxis Magazine.

Interview questions and answers follow:

Give a brief overview of how you were attracted to, and became involved in Mystery Spiritual Systems?

I first became interested in deeper levels of spirituality as I explored the tenants of Christianity. I went from attending Baptist church services with my aunt as a child, to having a step-father that was a loose version of a "Nationalist Muslim." I attended a Catholic high school after being kicked out of the public school system, and chose to be baptized Pentecostal while in undergrad. My wife, who at the time was my friend, invited me to my first African ceremony; an Egbe of the Yoruba tradition.

    I eventually became a Rastafarian, a tradition that introduced me to the deeper, mystical, and esoteric aspects of Christianity and an African perspective of the Bible and the religion as a whole. As a Rasta, I was taught of the importance of Ethiopia as a religious and spiritual center, but couldn't understand the aversion many Rastas had for Egypt and anything Egyptian, so naturally, I began to seek out and study the Egyptian culture and spirituality. I was able to teach many of my Rastafarian Bredren in the Caribbean the power of reconciling their disdain for the "biblical Egypt" by embracing the historically and culturally African Egypt. This added a practical element to the spiritual practices of my Rasta friends in the Caribbean. I had several deep and powerful spiritual experiences while performing rituals there with the Bobo Ashanti Rastafarians, as well as on my own up in the hills.

From there, I began to study Kemetic/Egyptian spiritual philosophy on a deeper level and began to practically apply what I found to be important and beneficial.

What is a Mystery School?

There are various definitions and interpretations of "Mystery Schools." One simple statement is that the mystery is simply "my-story," as opposed to history or "his-story." This simple statement is used in reference to how so much of what we, as African descendants, currently believe is attributed to European or Greco-Roman origins. This is especially true in regards to spirituality, science, fraternal organizations, medicine, etc. The mystery is the unknown contributions of our Ancestors, the teachings of which were contained in these so-called Mystery Schools. They were/are nothing more than the systems of spiritual initiation carried out amongst indigenous peoples worldwide. They were only mysterious to those who could not gain, or simply had not gained, entrance for whatever reason.

What are the African Spiritual Systems?

These are synonymous to the mystery systems...it is the practical application of what is learned while being initiated, and further perfected by the living of one's life, with the newfound perspective and orientation to, and with, reality. The spiritual expressions of Africa vary from region to region, group to group, and culture to culture. However, the underlying spiritual philosophy and overall worldview remains the same. This is why you can find direct correlations between spiritual concepts and principles found in East Africa with those found in Northern, Southern and Western Africa. The systemic nature is found in the organized structure, the specific rites, and the formulaic approach to addressing specific situations. It is not a haphazard, superstition-based method; instead, it is a well-documented, time tested, cornucopia of scientifically applied understanding.

What is the Kemetic Mystery System?

Some claim the Kemetic Mystery Systems to be the oldest in the world, however the Ancient Egyptians themselves gave credit to their Ancestors further up the Nile River, towards the interior of Africa. The Kemetic Mysteries have received so much attention in part because they left such an amazing record, encoded in such an intriguing fashion that archaeologists, anthropologists, and linguists have unsuccessfully sought to conquer her mysteries for centuries, if not millenia. The Kemetic spiritual systems seem to be a collection of universal truths, structured in such a way that anyone pursuing mastery along these lines will become a more efficient and effective human, capable of not only mastering their own person, but also mastering all of creation. The "mysteries" are how Ancient Egyptians were able to do what they did, and why modern humans can't figure it out. It requires a very specific worldview; an outlook, conceptualization and perception of reality that allows for the experiencing of the world in a deeper, mystical, and almost fantastical manner. The person operating from this worldview is like the scientist who has used a microscope compared to one that has no idea of the microbial world... they know of and can conceive of things that others cannot even fathom, based on their current understandings of reality.

What is the lineage of the Modern Mystery School?

As with Freemasonry, no one can pinpoint its actual origins with absolute certainty. Based on their [Ancient Egyptians] own records, they came from "the Foothills of the Mountains to the Moon" which is up river. Biblically, one could trace the lineage of the Kemetic Mysteries through the Hebrew scriptures and birthing the Hebrew culture and mystical sciences found in the Kabala, Zohar, and their many other esoteric traditions. It has already been made plain that the Greco-Roman societies also based their systems on those found in North East Africa, and thus, every European civilization that is based on the Greco-Roman philosophy is also directly traceable to those of the African continent. Then there is the story of Scota, an Egyptian princess, who settled and named Scotland. We also have the indisputable evidence found on both the North and South American continents of the African mystery systems in the form of temple pyramids, iconography, and linguistic similarities.

On the African continent, you can find a continuation of the Kemetic mysteries amongst the various groups who trace their Ancestral lineage to the Nile Valley. Africans have NEVER not initiated their priesthood... even amongst the great destruction of enslavement and colonialism; thus, there was never a time where the Mysteries were "lost" or dormant. Several European historians and archaeologists have written about their attempts to penetrate and even disrupt this esoteric transmission of spiritual initiation, only to find themselves falling short...even if they were victorious in specific instances.

Why do Mystery Schools exist?

From my understanding, Mystery Schools exist as a sort of living vessel for the preservation and transfer of knowledge from one generation to the next. They serve to keep an unbroken chain for communicating knowledge and wisdom from the beginning until the end of existence. Initiates of the mysteries are known as the caretakers of creation, and see to it that certain things remain known to humankind, even if the majority are ignorant of what the Truth actually is.

What would you consider to be the defining qualities of a Mystery School?

They must maintain a tradition of actualizing the human potential, along spiritual lines, according to a set protocol that has been carried on by the Ancients. These protocols vary widely on the surface, from culture to culture, but ultimately boil down to the EXACT same universal truths. It can be found in ALL VSLs. The signs of the authenticity of the Mystery school is found in its pupils...how do they function and manifest themselves?

Is it true that the teachings of the mystery schools contain the innermost knowledge of life and these teachings are deeply rooted in the old shamanic knowledge and ways of wisdom?

Yes, as far as I understand. My experiences have demonstrated this to me beyond the shadow of a doubt. Modern science is on a mission to catch up to this knowledge and is why major pharmaceutical companies spend money studying the "bush doctors" in the Amazon and other regions, trying to figure out what these "shamans" know, and how it can be "medicalized," "Westernized," and thus, monetized.

At what period in time or era did people stop living by the teachings, and thinking and acting according to certain ways of the Mystery Schools?

They have never gone dormant. There is ALWAYS a critical mass living according to these ways. What has happened is that we haven't seen entire civilizations based on these teachings, openly and beneficially, since the days of ancient and great civilizations such as those of the Nile Valley. The United States of America is said to be a civilization based on the Mysteries, however, the masses of her citizenship are not initiated and thus, are incapable of consciously/intentionally participating in the direction of the nation.

Did the Mystery Schools have an influence on Freemasonry, especially esoteric Freemasonry?

Absolutely. Freemasonry is one of those living vessels for the carrying on of the supreme truth and wisdom as shared amongst all other Mystery Schools. It's just that the majority of us have no clue what we possess. This is in part because we are still waking up from that "death blow," delivered by the Ruffians who sought to steal the Word and Way from us. This is why understanding the origins of Prince Hall Freemasonry as AFRICAN LODGE Freemasonry is so important. It points us in the direction needed to further unlock the sealed wisdom that has been held captive and only recently re-presented to us. It is equally important, for those of us interested in reclaiming our masonic greatness, to resist the urge to separate "esoteric" masonry from the social, political, educational, and whatever other forms of masonry we juxtapose against the "esoteric." According to the African and Mystery School tradition, there is no real separation...only the illusion that they are separate.

What questions do the deeper teachings of Mystery Schools help us answer?

Perhaps the most important questions are those that relate to our identity as human beings...demonstrating "who" and "what" we actually are; locating us in space and time with the questions "when" and "where;" and giving us a sense of divine purpose with the question "why," and the processes that will ensure that we live up to all of this with the question "how."

What is the brief history of the African Mystery Schools and their effect on the African Continent and civilization?

Many use the "human migration routes" to also trace the advance of civilization, which also includes the proliferation of the so-called "Mystery Schools." In almost every known civilization on this planet, there exists, or has existed, a method for maximizing human potential and transmitting the knowledge to do so. The continent of Africa has civilizations who boast of maintaining the systems designed by their Ancient Ancestors who migrated from the Nile Valley to other regions. The Dogon of

Mali are a perfect living example. In fact, one of the Smithsonian Museums recently had an exhibit highlighting the "Mud Masons of Mali," and their blend of spiritual science with their masonry. In short, EVERYTHING that has been accomplished by Africans, both continental and diasporic, by way of their spirituality and cultures has been made possible by the adherents to their Mystery Schools. It is what continues to attract foreign nations to African soil…although it is guised as a strict quest for their material resources; again, there is no separation of the material and the spiritual.

As an initiate of a number of Mystery Schools including several on the African Continent, what transformation and growth have you experience?

Having been initiated and advanced in several African schools of initiation has afforded me an opportunity to explore and experience reality in a way that many non-initiates may only inconsistently or sporadically experience. Just like in our Craft, initiates of other orders are also "made" prior to ever formally joining the order; they too are first prepared in their h_____. This means that we are all preordained to travel these paths, even if we never make the conscious and free-will decision to do so. There are many African "initiates" walking around "uninitiated;" either because they have avoided answering the call or they have failed to recognize the opportunity whenever it has shown itself.

Prior to being formally initiated, my life was filled with mystical experience (many of which I fully recognize in hindsight). Unfortunately, many of us are not born to parents who understand the spiritual sciences of our Ancestry, and thus, they are not equipped to foster the growth and development of the same in their children. As a result, we end up haphazardly going through life; blindly stumbling upon the road of life/initiation. Once I took my first initiation, everything became clear as day. My sense of purpose was strengthened, and my path made clear.

Is this a goal of Kemetic Mystery Systems?

Yes. The Kemetic Mystery System is thought to be one of the most Ancient human sources of Wisdom. It consists of a step-by-step blueprint of reality and how humans can most efficiently and effectively: maximize their potential, navigate/master the world of the living, and safely navigate the world that comes next.

Did the ancient Greeks get their ideas from the Africans?

Absolutely...there is no doubt about this. Anyone who professes otherwise is either intentionally trying to deceive OR they are ignorant to the facts.

What is your status or position as a Priest?

I am initiated as a Priest of Olokun in the Ifa tradition, found amongst the Yoruba in Nigeria and in Benin. I have been initiated, although not to the level of a functioning "priest" in both the Ewe and Jolla spiritual sciences found in Ghana and Gambia, respectively. I have also received priesthood initiation in a Kemetic Spiritual order. I am ranked to perform certain rites and rituals.

How many visits have you made to the African Content and what countries did you visit?

I have visited the African continent 4 times, including visits to: Gambia, Senegal, Ghana, Ivory Coast, and Benin.

What is your experience in reading hieroglyphics?

I took a non-traditional route to learning how to engage the hieroglyphic language. Before I sought to learn how to read the symbols in a written, letter-for-symbol fashion, as taught by most Western schools of thought, I learned how to shift my perspective and paradigm in regards to understanding the spiritual sciences employed by the civilization and culture that created and used the language. After being well developed in these aspects of the sciences, I then went and became formally trained in the linguistics of the Egyptian hieroglyphs at a University, under the guidance of a professor who has been teaching the language for over 20 years. I would rate myself an early beginner.

Many mistakenly believe that a person CANNOT have an understanding of the Kemetic Spiritual Science WITHOUT learning the language; and conversely, because they know the language they automatically have a superior understanding of the science... that is not true.

There are many who can boast of being able to "read" the hieroglyphs, but have little TRUE understanding and interpretation of the symbolism found therein. They give a PURELY intellectual treatment to the science and thus, become arrogant in their command of information, with very little evidence of Wisdom and Understanding. They will then make presumptuous statements like: "No one knows what the Kemetic Mystery Schools were..." or "The Kemetic language was lost until Champollion 'discovered' the Rosetta Stone." Like most things, this type of person gives an intellectual treatment to sciences that are based on principles and tools that reach far beyond intellectualism, and therefore, their ability to understand.

Has your experience in Mystery Schools helped with your Masonic travels?

My African initiations have definitely helped me in my Masonic travels. These experiences have afforded me a rare level of insight into our Craft and have given me the use of practical tools and experiences that the average Brother may not even know exist. Certain veils are lifted with every true initiation, and thus the initiated are able to access things that those who remain behind the veil are incapable of knowing/understanding. One of my African priesthood initiations took place AFTER my being Raised. In fact, the African high priest overseeing my initiation was also a MM, 32nd Degree, and a Knight's Templar. We were able to talk about both traditions from a vantage point that many have yet to fathom.

Based on my knowledge of African Spiritual Science, I am able to now look at our Masonic symbols in a new Light; a Light more consistent with what our Founding 15 originally called our branch of Freemasonry...the African Lodge. I am able to take our Masonic Allegories and Symbols, and unearth the embedded rituals that allow us to truly make good men better, and to advance our understanding of our Craft. For example, I have taught the "Rough Ashlar Ritual," as transmitted by a Trinidadian Brother who is also initiated as an African priest...you'd be amazed at its simplicity and effectiveness.

Finally, please provide your symbolic interpretation of the image we are planning to use on the cover of this issue of the Phylaxis Magazine.

It is a very complex symbol, with many, many layers of interpretation. On one level, the sun disk with the serpent is considered to be the initial active manifestation of reality. The serpent is in an active state which symbolizes a conscious intention behind the use of the creative energy identified by the sun. This conscious intention is first set into motion by the Creator of All, and serves as the initial cause of all other causes and their subsequent effects. The sun, being the sustainer of life in our solar system, gives off an infinite and undetermined amount of energy/substance that is used by EVERY living thing on our planet (even those creatures that dwell deep within caves and/or on the ocean floor benefit indirectly from the sun's energy). It is this initial active manifestation that gives life to everything. It is the source of the initial heartbeat; the initial spark that gets the nervous system activated; the force that inspires the seed to sprout, molecules to speed up, water to flow, eggs to hatch, and the planets to rotate and revolve. It is the movement of life.

The rays are the various pathways through which life force travels to the various things that are the recipients of this vital force, in their various ways. It is similar to how the spectrum of light goes well beyond what is visible by human eyes, and how the properties of light go well beyond illumination. Each individual ray extending from the sundisk carries exactly what is needed to whatever needs it; indiscriminately providing for all. This particular version of the sundisk (Aten) was made popular by Amenhotep IV (1350-1334 BC), who changed his name to Akhenaten and elevated Aten over the priesthood of Amen during his reign. The artistic expression of Kemetic culture also took a shift during his reign to include a distinct way of representing the human form.

      In regards to the words, what I see is the word for a student of the mysteries, which is simultaneously a keeper of the mysteries, Seba (although the Medu seem to spell out Sebai(y)t, which is simply a variation of Seba). This concept deals with a portal through which wisdom and high knowledge is brought into consciousness. Seba is literally a star, and gives the idea that our Ancestors understood the stars to be portals through which energy and consciousness traveled to those who have been duly prepared to receive; this is exactly what is portrayed by the sun disk (which is also a star) in the earlier explanation. The scroll at the end of the word denotes specific wisdom teachings that are to be imparted by a Master to their pupil. In true African fashion, it is impossible to separate the teachings from the life of those being taught; once instructed, the true initiate becomes a living example of that teaching. They no longer simply possess information, but are now complete embodiments and sacred vessels for that wisdom to survive. This is who we are as Prince Hall Freemasons. The carriers of the wisdom of our Great Ancestors. For those of us who have yet to seek deeper into Mysteries hinted at by our Founding Fifteen when they called us the African Lodge, we are like unfortified vessels, allowing the information to not be contained and thus not assimilated into our daily walks. It is time that we fortify and live up to our Ancestral expectations and honor their sacrifice.

An African Rite Considered

Jeff Menzise, Ph.D., 32°, FPS

*H*onorable Brothers, I hereby present to you, the Craft, a synopsis of what I have received during my meditations as a viable option for building upon those foundation stones laid by our Founding Fifteen[1]. It is my perspective that, with all things in Freemasonry, the word African as found in the original title for Prince Hall Freemasonry can be used as a symbol from which we can draw more Masonic Light. Not only is this Light beneficial as a supplement to our pursuits as Free-Masons, but it is central to our core dispositions as descendants of the African Lodge.

When I speak of an African Rite, I am speaking of a Rite comparable to the York and the Scottish, where the rituals reflect the culture and spirituality of African peoples; with Africans as the main actors of the dramas, allegories, and myths. I have considered the fact that there are many Lodges found throughout the continent of Africa, many of which were established by European colonists. And although it is likely that the ritual performed in these Lodges is almost always the ritual of Europe, they can carry the name of an African country or cultural group. This may confuse some into believing that the ritual was actually African in its worldview. One great and readily available example of this is found in the *Nigerian Ritual* compiled by Brother C. M. Browne, M.C., O.B.E., the Deputy District Grand Master of Nigeria in the 1930s.

What Brother Browne has compiled is the version of Masonic Ritual taught in the *Emulation Lodge of Improvement*, which met at Freemason's Hall in London. The ritual, as it existed at the time of the compiling, is what Brother Tasker taught as he toured Nigeria in 1936. Brother Browne felt the need to provide a written copy of the "Emulation Ritual" to compensate for the few numbers of qualified instructors of

Masonic ritual amongst the Lodges found in Nigeria. As a point of reiteration, one must not confuse the title of "Nigerian Ritual" to be anything other than a label identifying where on the African continent the European-based Masonic ritual was being practiced. Additionally, some may cite this document as evidence that African-based Freemasonry followed the same rituals as European-based Freemasonry. While in some cases this may be true. Based on my conversations with African Freemasons under these systems, there is still an African-based worldview that filters how these African Masons engage the European ritual and their ability to use these rituals in an African way. This is done by infusing a pre-existing African ritual with the newly introduced European ritual system and concepts.

In fact, during my stay in Gambia, West Africa, I spent considerable amounts of time in a particular village with a host family. One of my dear friends, also from the United States, lived with a separate host family. While visiting him in their compound, we dialogued with the patriarch of his host family who primarily spoke French, amongst his various other African tongues. There was a young lady serving as translator for us. At some point in our discussion, we began to converse about African spirituality. Lamen, our host, began to speak of his perspectives. As he spoke, I continually heard one word that stood out amongst the mostly incomprehensible languages he spoke. That word was "Mason."

    He detailed how he grew up in Senegal within the Mandinkan tradition, and how he became a Mason, as his forefathers were. The Masonry he spoke of was quite distinct from the Speculative Masonry we currently embrace. It was a fusion of both the Operative and the Speculative Crafts. It was more holistic. He proudly spoke of how he built the very compound in which we currently sat. He gestured towards the many charms and amulets on his arms, his rings, and the necklaces draped around his neck. These all contained very specific and very powerful magic, some of which were demonstrated to us by literally placing the charms and amulets on our person, and feeling the works. I have pictures of some of these trials, and left the continent with my

An African Rite Considered

share of spiritual "juju."

Lamen took us to meet with the village Maribou, who demonstrated for us how he created these charms. We watched as he drew symbols on pieces of paper; some totally unrecognizable, others were configurations of various Arabic words styled in very precise and particular patterns. These papers were either stuffed down into a small goat horn, to be worn on the arm, or twisted tightly into a small leather pouch to be worn around the neck. There was even a cloth belt, incrementally knotted, with cowrie shells fitted at each node, to be tied around the waist. On a later trip to Ghana, I had this "juju" upgraded from an external compendium, to an internal force. My spiritual guide had me discard these items as a demonstration of faith in my internal growth and development and the guidance that God has given me thus far in life. This faith was tested, and proven true in both Gambia and Ghana. I briefly illustrate this in Symbolically Speaking, Vol. 1.

We find a continuation of the cloaking of traditional African spirituality in the more "modern" spiritual traditions such as Voudoun, Santaria, and many forms of worship adjacent to the Black Church, especially those in the rural South. Even if the ceremonies are exactly the same in form, the expression and thus the function may differ. This is exemplified by enslaved Africans singing church hymns, concealing plans for escape and/or clandestine meetings. It is further exemplified by the quilting mothers of the south, who wove stories and instructions into the fabrics to be worn by their messengers. They adapted to the necessity of their then-current situation, used the tools and means afforded them by their circumstance, and infused their knowledge into the crafts given to them.

The "early" African Masons who may have participated in the European Lodges found on the African continent, did so in much the same way. They could not automatically "shut off" the way they understand the world to be. Even the ones who totally wanted to abandon their African worldview, could not instantly do so. They could feign disgust and abandonment of their indigenous cultural expressions

An African Rite Considered

maintained by others, but internally, the understanding of the ritual and rites of their fellow African was understood. This is just how worldview works. Eventually over time, they could loosen their adherence to the ways of their Ancestors; even still, it remained at their core. Much of this has to do with the fact that Africans and Europeans have a largely differing worldview[2].

In other words, the axiology (values), epistemology (how knowledge is acquired), ontology (the nature of reality), and other cultural dynamics, requires that each of these collective groups perceive and experience the world differently, and thereby, engage the world (including nature, other people, the Supreme Being, etc.) in very different ways. The importance of this point cannot be expressed enough. Thus, we will take some time to discuss worldview as it relates to axiology, ontology, and epistemology. In <u>Symbolically Speaking, Vol. 1</u>, I wrote:

> For those of African genetic descent, specifically those of more recent African ancestry who continue to carry the phenotypes of their African ancestors,

the Hebrew-based symbolism of the Masonic allegories of today, serves the purpose of transmitting certain messages and enlightening the initiated through their use. This symbolism is effective, however, I maintain that there is a more powerful and spiritually relevant set of allegories and symbols that will better serve Seekers who are descendants of the African Lodge (keeping in mind that the process is designed to be transformative).[3]

...The depth found in our use of symbolism is either strengthened or weakened in direct relationship to the worldview by which we engage them, and thus, it is important for us to seek an understanding of the general ontology[4] found on the African continent. Yes, there are many, many cultures found on the African continent, however it has been well demonstrated that at the core of each, their worldviews are basically the same.

Let us first explore the notion that our Masonic initiation process is designed to be transformative. The first dimension of transformation is the psychological. The concept of psychology is very deep and complex and happens to be my profession and field of expertise. Looking at the etymology, we see that psychology is actually the "study of the soul," however, for the sake of this discussion, we will deal with the definition given in the related end note, i.e., "changes in understanding of self." Generally speaking, the understanding that we have about ourselves, as human beings is continually changing. However, this change is often limited and bound within a set parameter; meaning this change typically only occurs within preset boundaries, defined by the individual's worldview, as well as the time and effort put forward in their quest for self-knowledge.

This is like a person who has one acre of land to farm. They can make all the changes they want, within that one acre. They can build and till the soil right up to the boundaries. They can dig deeper and deeper, or build taller and taller, but it must remain on that one acre of land. Compare this to the rest of the available land on earth; it is but a crumb fallen from the pound cake. The person with 15 acres is likewise bound by their limits, although their limits are broader and wider. Having the expanded boundaries does not necessarily guarantee that they will cover more ground. Instead, the 15-acre owner could develop but ½ an acre, leaving the rest to be overgrown.

Let's say, as a practical example, a person's self-concept is that they are a "born sinner," and this concept is directly related to their religious orientation. The religion has defined the boundaries of their worldview as it relates to their self-concept, and has likely defined the path for finding redemption. This may also determine the means by which knowledge is pursued, the sources that are deemed valid (and those that must be avoided), how self-improvement is defined, as well as the possibilities and realities of what this self can even be. Additionally, anything that contradicts the belief that humans are born sinners is then discredited and perhaps devalued by the individual who ascribes to this perspective (of course it depends on how strongly they hold to this view).

An African Rite Considered

Furthermore, any form of knowing that occurs beyond the scope of the prescribed boundaries are either considered invalid, or otherwise off limits and negative. One example of this type of knowledge is astrology and/or astronomy. Many modern religions restrict their followers from using astrology and/or astronomy as a means for understanding life's circumstances, even though the religions themselves are filled with astrological signs and symbols. It is sometimes invalidated as a charlatan's tool, or even as something wicked and demonic. Thus, the devoted adherent has been cut-off from the deeper aspects of their own religion, and an entire world of knowledge and tools that have assisted humans on their quest for generations.

This is directly related to ontology, i.e., the study and nature of reality; and epistemology—the study of knowledge and justified beliefs. How one views reality and how knowledge is acquired determines, to a large extent, their path of growth and development. Even the value placed on these two variables has a major impact on people. In our above example, this person may become more proficient and knowledgeable regarding how humans work towards their redemption as sinners, and even how they can counteract the "natural tendencies" to sin.

They will likely, consciously or unconsciously, describe and explain things that occur in life, along these lines, even to the point of expecting people to sin in a helpless manner because it is their *nature* to do so. If this particular religion has prescribed dates, times, locations, sources, and authorities, associated with the pursuit of this knowledge, then the person may limit their search to these parameters. The exception is usually found amongst those who are seeking to become leaders within these organizations and institutions. They are more likely to study deeper, and more broadly within the existing parameters. There are even some who will search outside of the boundaries; in statistics, we call these outliers, the exceptions to the "norm." This is the Mason who seeks "Light outside of the Lodge."

For the sake of perspective, let's also look at the person whose self-concept is that humans are born as divine beings. Exactly as with the previous example, this individual's paradigm and parameters are predefined and may also be related to a particular religion. The major difference here is in the subject of exploration, as well as in one's orientation towards their human potential. This worldview is likely to set the individual on a quest to understand what it means to be a divine being. Along this trajectory, they may also embark upon a journey to discover how to actualize and make practical the various aspects of divinity in their daily lives.

The real-world example of this perspective exists in the many spiritual traditions that focus on evolving adherents to their highest spiritual potential. You find this throughout the continent of Africa, you can find it in the traditions of India, and amongst the many indigenous cultures around the world. Central to this perspective is the idea of divinity; thus, a seeker must develop a clear concept of what it means to be divine. In almost every recorded religion on the planet, there exist examples of divine men and women on this path to model and learn from.

      The above discourse demonstrates how each perspective overlaps, and how they can yield the similar results, i.e., the spiritual development of the person beyond their basic cognitive and physical functioning. Intellectually it makes sense for one to recognize the relationship of the two. Prior to this discourse, it is likely that many have never looked at the two in tandem. Similar to how one rarely thinks of the converse perspective of the THEORY of evolution which states, in part, that humans and apes evolved from a common ancestor, based on similarities in DNA.

      This perspective means that Africans, who are now promoted as the first humans on the planet, are not so far-removed from apes on the evolutionary scale, and that the more recent humans, Europeans, are the newest, more highly evolved version. A perspective to juxtapose against the theory of human evolution is one that I like to call the "Theory of Descending." This perspective states that humans descended from God; meaning we have our origins in the Most High and share the same-similar qualities and characteristics of GAOTU, although in vastly different quantities, with varying degrees of mastery.

Like a drop of water compared to the ocean, both are made of H_2O, but in obviously different quantities. And due to the vastness of the ocean, there are far greater things contained within its waters, and the energies of the oceans are far superior to those that can fit into a mere drop. However, as demonstrated by modern chemistry, there is great power contained within even a single molecule of H_2O (i.e., The H-Bomb).

The former perspective (evolution) measures human growth and progress based on intellectual and technological advances, which typically also decreases their humanity. The latter perspective (divine descendants) identifies how far we have fallen in direct proportion to how little we know of our spiritual selves and the inefficiency in applying our spiritual tools; and an adherence to the fragmented approach to life. For example, some blame the global energy and resource crisis on the "over-population" of the planet, advocating for various tactics of population control. The reality of this truly perilous situation is that resources are being mined and used in a very inefficient manner, producing more waste, destruction, and pollution than is necessary. These two perspectives, evolution and descending, are literally the inverse of one another.

      As we have learned in the symbolism of the "Star of David," the two overlapping triangles with one peak pointing upwards while the other points down, Man is a combination of both the physical and spiritual aspects of being human; both descending and evolving. Similar to how our S_____ and C_____s interact, the degree of efficiency and effectiveness on either level, is symbolized by how the instruments are positioned. Operating as animals (animated creatures), seeking to redeem ourselves as sinners, typically keeps the spiritual subservient to the physical passions and innate reactions of the body, emotions, and intellect. Operating as divine beings places the physical aspects submissive to, and beneath, our spiritual dictates. This suggests, for some, that the spiritual is superior to that of the physical. Some argue that neither is superior to the other, and that we should work to "balance" the physical and spiritual; I agree.

My perspective of what this "balance" looks like, may differ from the typical person presenting this argument. For example, if I were to place an ounce of wheat flour on one side of a scale and attempted to balance it with solid gold, there would be much more wheat flour on the scale than there would be gold, strictly in regards to quantity and perhaps even volume (depending on how the gold is shaped). Yes, the weight is the same, but the volume and perhaps quantity will differ. Just as it may take 15 grapes to equal the weight of one grapefruit. In other words, it would take an uneven number of units to balance out the two weights—yet, it is balanced.

In regards to balancing the spiritual and physical aspects of our selves, the physical concerns are equally as important as the spiritual concerns, while differing greatly. The spiritual and physical exist on two ends of the same continuum, and depending on the order of operations, developing the physical will yield very different results than development of the spiritual. There are schools of thought for each extreme and all points in-between. To elaborate on more than one or two of these will take us too far from the point of this chapter. Suffice it to say: where one places focus, determines the path taken.

Some people focus greatly on physical development, and the mastery of their physical body. Others place the bulk of their focus on mastering the spiritual. These individuals live in a more detached way from the physical parts of reality. There are even people who start with either a physical or spiritual focus, then gravitate towards the development of the other. Believe it or not, there are even those who totally neglect both; imagine that. Finally, there are those who are fortunate enough to develop the two simultaneously. The physical is developed for the sake of the spiritual, and the spiritual is developed to more efficiently and effectively interact with the physical. They are correctly viewed as two sides of the same coin.

An African Rite Considered

At different phases of our development, humans oscillate between where their internal, energetic, and psychological focus is targeted. Sigmund Freud identified this in his psychosexual stages of human development. He noted that early in life, the developing human's main "concern" is their physical development, literally the building of their body: organs, physical abilities, etc. This concern is addressed and tended to by focusing on oral stimulation and the placing of objects in the mouth. This signifies the desire to ingest nutritious substances for the purpose of satisfying hunger as well as to develop the physical body towards a state of self-sufficiency.

Freud called this the "Oral" stage, wherein the body's "life force" or libido is focused on the place of most importance for that stage of development: towards oral gratification and physical satiation. The person who has developed in a relatively healthy manner during this phase may feel satisfied and fulfilled. They typically will not feel a need to hoard and covet. On the other end, people who may have experienced challenges at this stage of growth and development, may exhibit an "oral fixation," needing to always have something in their mouth. This can translate into overeating, smoking, and chewing on pens.

In his next stage, the Anal, Freud identified the need to control defecation and maintain a certain level of cleanliness, as the primary focus. This is the period when humans typically become "potty trained" and no longer need the use of diapers. Control of our body's functions and directing how needs are fulfilled, are two major opportunities afforded the child at this stage. This is also where some begin to become "anal retentive" or even form aspects of an obsessive-compulsive disorder.

Control of the anal sphincter means one no longer has to walk around in their own bodily waste; this is a major accomplishment and has deep and lasting effects on one's social life, confidence, and a sense of security and desirability. According to this theoretical perspective, pleasure derived from self-mastery is always the motivating force behind these various stages of development. It is how we experience the various stages—successfully or in failure, with ease or with great tribulation, with external support or in isolation—that determines the formation of our adult personalities and our perspectives and methods for interacting with the world.

His third stage, Phallic, is where the individual begins to identify the physical basis for gender differences between the two sexes, male and female. This is where children are often found exploring and comparing their bodies with other children of both the same and opposite sex. This is also where Freud theorized children develop the Elektra and Oedipal complexes. These theoretical complexes identify a phase wherein children are attracted to the parent of the opposite sex and begin to imitate the characteristics of the same sex parent as a means of reducing the tension generated by their desire.

Many criticized Freud heavily for insinuating that children at this very young age have a sexual desire for their adult parents. His perspective, from my vantage point, was limited by the worldview through which he functioned, and perhaps the ones criticizing him, are limited in their understanding of what he actually meant. His studies into spirituality (psychology) led both he and Carl G. Jung into various non-Western cultures including those of Africa. They came upon societies and worldviews that were designed to operate holistically, and were based on dual-hemispheric brain operations and perspectives. Being limited by their own worldview and culture of origins, they, Jung and Freud, were limited in their ability to know, understand, and translate the perspectives of their respected teachers, and thus were only capable of bringing back fragmented duplications of the lessons they learned.

As a result of these limitations, both were greatly tormented in life, frustrated by this inability to grasp the sophisticated truths discovered and guarded by these various cultures, who were falsely accused of being inferior to the cultures of Europe. This created great cognitive dissonance[5], which in turn led to the great controversy and shaming of them by colleagues. The balanced and perhaps more accurate view of how sexuality plays a part in human development is found in "Eastern" perspectives, which propose that the life-force energy (Kundalini, Chi, Qi, Ra, Libido) is the same force expressed and channeled in all other aspects of life. The "sex-drive" is actually the "drive" to grow and expand the individual's personal life, and their space and place in the world. This is done both by creation via sexual reproduction and creation via the sublimation of this sex drive, converting it into the industrious application of one's cognitive abilities.[6]

    His fourth stage, Latency, is where the libido seems to retreat a bit from the foreground and the person begins to focus on their intellectual and social interactions. Having friends and being a welcomed part of social groups, organizations, teams, etc., is very important at this phase of development. This is typically where boys become "gross" to girls, and girls are "stupid" to boys. Each finds solace in their own gender group and "learns" from others what it is to be male or female.

    In traditional societies, this is the period where children experience their "rites of passage" initiations. It is the pre-pubescent rites that prepares them for life as an adult whose reproductive capabilities are about to awaken, both physiologically and psychologically. Understanding that all things have polarity, including humans, we can better comprehend how this latency stage helps to "ground" boys and girls in their specific "pole," and how the previous and subsequent stages used the polarity of the complementary sex to drive growth and development.

    In Freud's final stage of psycho-sexual development, the growing human emerges into what is called the Genital stage. This is where adulthood is said to formally begin. The idea is that both the male and female have entered into puberty and are now capable of physically reproducing. The attraction for the opposite sex is now present and is driven by the increase of sex hormones and the development of the sex and reproductive organs in both. Without the proper guidance, mentioned as "rites of passage" in the earlier example, many young adults are left to fend for themselves. This can lead to a warped sense of sexuality, adulthood, and a likely squandering of the vital life-force (Libido, Qi, Chi, Kundalini), all of which impact an individual's capacity to function as a healthy and well-adapted citizen.

Again, Freud's stages have been used as an example of how worldview can, and does, shape and skew knowledge and perspective. His stages are also examples of how this knowledge is used to shape and skew the self-concept maintained by those who adhere to this particular perspective of what it is to be a human and how we develop. There are many counter-theories, some of which focus more on the cognitive development of humans, others focus on the biological development of humans, while still others focus on the ecological or environmental influences on the developing human being. As mentioned at the outset of this discussion, each perspective sets the boundaries of the worldview through which the individual engages and interprets the world.

The next point in our list of transformation is "convictional," which is defined as: revisions in one's belief system. Beliefs are an interesting phenomenon to ponder. On one extreme they are very fragile and fickle, while on the other extreme they are strong enough to motivate and lead people to slaughter millions. To believe, intellectually speaking, is different from a feeling; it differs from thinking, and it also differs from knowing. An illustration I often use when teaching the difference between believing, thinking, feeling, and knowing follows:

> *You come to a parking lot and attempt to start your car. The key turns but the car does not start. Someone comes along and says he **believes** the problem is with your starter and that you should go buy one immediately and have it installed. Another person comes along and says, "I **think** it may be your battery. You should buy one and have them install it as soon as possible." A third person then comes along and tells you "I **feel** like the problem is in your ignition system. You should get your switches checked and changed out." Finally, a fourth person comes along and says, "I **know** what the problem is, you need to put some gas directly into the carbu-*

retor and it will start right up." For the sake of this example, each individual is telling the truth about their position: the one who thinks REALLY thinks his suggestion is true; the one who feels REALLY feels their suggestion is true; the one who believes REALLY believes their suggestion is true; and the one who knows REALLY knows their suggestion is true. Who do you follow? The believer, thinker, feeler, or knower?

The word science comes from the Latin "scio" which means "to know." Perhaps this is why there is a higher value placed on "science" than other forms and methods of knowing and dealing with information. This is why when someone wants to sound authoritative, especially in academia, they will say "Well science has determined that…" This does not mean that every scientist or every piece of scientific information is based squarely on knowledge, or that every scientist is free from following beliefs, thoughts, and feelings for the sake of finding and sharing pure knowledge.

On the contrary, many are still human beings with beliefs strong enough to override their quest for knowledge, even while proclaiming to be the most knowledgeable. The reality is, they have simply constructed a paradigm that encompasses and dictates the worldview of the masses of people. For example, the relatively recent separation of "science" from "magic" was based on the need to limit the types of knowledge to be explored and to separate the obvious connection between spirituality, knowledge, and political power. It's the reason why many ailments are never said to be cured, but only advertised as being "in remission," or "treated." And why people who claim and demonstrate that they are able to cure an "incurable" disease are often charged with a crime punishable by both monetary fines and jail time; even if they have a demonstrated track record of "curing" the "incurable" disease.

Science itself, is exactly what it is: knowledge. The trouble arises when people, with their own limitations and biases, begin to influence the valid means by which one obtains knowledge; in other words, how one knows what they know. This is epistemology; the study of the nature of knowledge and how one acquires it. It's almost as if "scientists" believe themselves to be personifications of science, forgetting their flaws in the process. This can sometimes lead to arrogance and in extreme cases, a "god-complex."

This leads us to the most profound revisions to be made in your belief system: your self-concept. Self-concept includes: who you believe you are, what you believe about your potential, what you believe about your value and worth as a person, what you believe about your potential and capabilities, and what you believe about your purpose for being born. For the majority of people, it is safe to say that they have limiting beliefs in these areas. The average person does not spend time exploring these perspectives in depth, and thus, are likely to be lacking in understanding in this regard. Test this out for yourself. Ask a person (yourself) the following questions: Who do you believe you are? What is your potential in life? What is your value and worth as a person? What is your life's purpose? Some will have answers, others may not. Some answers may make sense and be elaborate, others may be short, simple to the point and of sound reason. It will vary. Regardless, everyone will benefit from the exploration of these questions and an earnest seeking of answers on ever-deepening levels.

In the current context of racism/White supremacy, much of what is presented as high culture and high science is designed to uplift the image and concept of Whites, while demeaning and belittling, even if just by exclusion, the importance, value, and worth of non-Whites. You can find evidence of this in all areas of people activity, including: economics, education, entertainment, labor, law, politics, religion, sex, and war.

This is even true in our Masonic ritual and mythology. As descendants from the African Lodge, we have kept with tradition and used the Hebrew-based mythology and legends to guide our Craft. Whenever we see images to reflect the characters in our stories, we are presented with Caucasians; almost always. Ideally, there is nothing wrong with this depiction except that it is culturally incorrect for the region in which many of the stories take place, and the fact that personalities such as King Solomon have been described as "black and comely." Every depiction of H.A. that I have ever seen, was that of a White male.

Although this is not a discussion on the color of Jesus, the Christ, we will use his popular depiction as an illustration to further the point introduced in the previous paragraph. According to Dr. Frances Cress Welsing, a world-renowned physician and psychiatrist:

> Absolutely critical to the white supremacy system of religious thought was the formation of the image of a white man as the "son" of God. This white male image then was referred to as "Christ" – no matter that the prophet Jesus was a Black man. Because the brain-computer functions most fundamentally on logic circuits, at deep unconscious levels it automatically computes that God, the father, is also a white male. If God is other than white, he would have produced a Black (or other non-white) son...

In other words, if in the deep, unconscious recesses of my brain-computer rests the fundamental logic that God is a white man and that I should worship "God," all of my attempts at liberation will move me only in a circle. Indeed, the circumference of my "liberation movement circle" could be so wide that it really appears to me that I am moving in a straight line of progress. But moving in a circle, no matter how big the circle, is tantamount to standing absolutely still, marking time. Many Black people in the U.S. now are beginning to feel as though our liberation efforts (in spite of loss of life and whipped heads) have left us still standing on the same spot of white oppression.

For the vast majority of Black and other non-white peoples today, the arrival of these ice cold facts of brain-computer logic at the conscious level will be experienced initially as shattering and self-disintegrating — primarily because it is God the protector and the creator upon whom the self is taught (programmed) ultimately to depend. If the concept of God is removed from my brain-computer, upon

An African Rite Considered

whom or what am I to lean, especially if I am feeling oppressed depressed and overwhelmed? If there is nothing or no one to provide support, then I believe I will collapse and disintegrate…

It might be instructive at this juncture to recall that Christianity was based upon the life and activity of an African (Black) prophet named Jesus. That the White Romans recognized this fact is reflected in the early portrayals of Jesus and his mother as the Black Madonna and Black child. To this day, a picture of the Black Madonna and Black child secretly is cherished as one of the most holy icons of the original Christian church, the Catholic church.

– Isis Papers, pp. 166-170

Similar to what Dr. Welsing is pointing out regarding the color of Jesus and the resulting psychological impact, the images that we use for our most esteemed and revered icons has an equally important impact on our subtle perceptions of ourselves and our "branch" of the Craft. In a recent conversation with one of our White Masonic Brothers, I shared my theory that somewhere in the distant past, after the Wisdom Traditions of Africa became the intellectual property of European "travelers," there was an agreement made that if the Africans and their descendants ever "woke up" and sought to reclaim their knowledge and wisdom (so-called Mystery Teachings), then it must be returned to them. The catch is that there was no requirement to show them how to use it. This has resulted in the plight of African Lodge Masons (now referred to as Prince Hall Freemasons), who have been in an on-going battle to establish legitimacy, credibility, and perhaps most importantly, themselves as a true Masonic body with a legacy as rich and worthy as those whose origins are traced to an English pub in 1717.

    I continued in my conversation by pointing out how it is clear that White Freemasons and Black Freemasons are obviously applying the Craft differently. All we have to do is take a look at the White Masonic Grand Lodges, the wealth they accumulate, and the power they maintain and control, compare it to ours and realize that something is vastly different. Are we moving in a large circle that seems to be a straight trajectory of progress? To this I say yes. Is the gaining of mutual recognition and visitation rights enough to garner enthusiastic celebration from us? To this, I say no. We would greatly benefit from declaring and holding steadfast to more lofty goals.

In all of our Prince Hall iconography, aside from the individual Brother(s) who may bridge their Masonic understanding with their cultural orientation, I have yet to see a true and clear honoring of anything African, aside from the name "African Lodge," related to and accepted by our PHA Craft, at large. Yet, in the mainstream lodges across this nation and the world, we can readily find entire Lodge rooms decorated and designed according to ancient African temples found along the Nile River. As mentioned earlier, almost every character in our Masonic mythology is depicted as a Caucasian. All of our Masonic myths seem to all originate from the European and/or Western worldview, according to the Judaic allegory and culture. Again, there is nothing inherently wrong with this because we are able to glean universal knowledge and wisdom from these tales, but what is the impact on our psyche, as discussed by Dr. Welsing? According to Joseph Campbell in his phenomenal work, <u>The Power of Myth</u>:

> Myths are clues to the spiritual potentialities of the human life...They teach you that you can turn inward, and you begin to get the message of the symbols. Read other people's myths, not those of your own religion, because you tend to interpret your own religion in terms of facts—but if you read the other ones, you begin to get the message. Myth helps you to put your mind in touch with this experience of being alive. It tells you what the experience is...Now, when these were dropped, a whole tradition of Occidental mythological information was lost. It used to be that these stories were in the minds of people. When the story is in your mind, then you see its relevance to something happening in your own life. It gives you perspective on what's happening to you. With the loss of that, we've really lost something because we don't have a comparable literature to take its place. These bits of information from ancient times, which have to do with the themes that have supported human

life, built civilizations, and informed religions over millennia, have to do with deep inner problems, inner mysteries, inner thresholds of passage, and if you don't know what the guide-signs are along the way, you have to work it out yourself.

As descendants of Africa and the African Lodge, we have lost our mythology and have adopted the stories that are befitting to others. When given lemons, we have made lemonade. Great. But what about all the other things that our stories contain? How would it benefit us to refine ourselves using the stories of our Ancestral legacy? In Joseph Campbell's statement, he suggests using the mythologies of others in order to glean the deeper messages, because to use one's own mythology, it may be misconstrued as fact-based information as opposed to allegory. In our case, what we claim as our own IS that of another, thus logically, it is the reclaiming of our own that will serve the same purpose as reading that of another. Oh, the paradox.

If you have been brought any discomfort while reading this section of the paper (or any of it for that matter), this is evidence of your beliefs being challenged, and is actually the point of the article, and is consistent with the second of the three characteristics of transformation. When we experience mental discomfort and become emotionally involved in the discussion or reading of a topic, it is usually an indication that something read or said has conflicted with a previously held belief and that there is a strong desire to hold on to, and, at all costs, defend that belief. There is nothing inherently wrong with this, in fact it is considered a natural part of the learning and growing process. However, when the reaction is "knee-jerk," and the mission is to disprove, discredit, or otherwise dismiss the "offending" information and its presenter, we begin to enter dangerous territory.

Many of us have witnessed conversations where a new perspective is presented and those who hold the old seek to attack and silence, by a multitude of means, the presenter of the new perspective. People will do this by attacking the person's character, they will attempt to find loopholes in the statements being made

An African Rite Considered

(even when these loopholes have absolutely nothing to do with the meaning of the message), some will even resort to deliberate deception and the invention of lies to get others to reject the perspective. Thomas Kuhn, in his book The Structure of Scientific Revolution, identified such behaviors as the paradigm attempting to preserve itself against the force of an anomaly.

If an anomaly goes unchecked, it will cause the current paradigm to shift, and thus many things will have to be lost or transformed in the process. Those who were once thought to be superior in knowledge, wisdom, and understanding, may be exposed as being propped up by flimsy straw scaffolds. Those who were once ridiculed as being ignorant and subject to fantasy, may be heralded as leaders of the new school of thought for scientific and social explorations. The old regime has a lot to lose, and thus are rightfully threatened by the existence of an anomaly within their current paradigms. In line with the following statement by Dr. Frances Cress Welsing, we, as descendants of the African Lodge, must fearlessly pursue Masonic Light in ways that work optimally for us, using systems, processes, mythologies, and rituals that are designed by us and according to our own worldview. Without these fundamental changes in our belief systems, we cannot truly experience the transformation promised by the rituals in our Craft.

> ...no matter what the level of initial trauma felt when this logic circuit is brought to conscious awareness, it must come fully to light and be yanked out. Indeed, there can be no mental health, self-respect or positive self-concept for Black or other non-White peoples as long as this specious and destructive logic circuit remains in place.
>
> – Isis Papers, p. 169

Let us now explore the third aspect of transformation: behavioral – changes in lifestyle. You can infer what a person thinks of themselves and what they believe based on what they do. Often times, self-concept and beliefs exist on a subconscious level of the mind so if you ask a person what they believe, they'll tell you what is in their conscious mind, while their true beliefs are knowable by watching their actions.

An African Rite Considered

It can get tricky, as demonstrated by high-level behavior psychologists. They are able to influence and manipulate the behaviors of unsuspecting people, without any concern for their beliefs and self-concepts. In fact, behavioral psychologists see the human as a programmable computer whose behaviors can be mechanically manipulated and induced. This is demonstrated by Pavlov's experiments, as well as those of Skinner. How often has someone pointed out something to you that you didn't realize you were doing? How often have you observed someone getting "defensive" when another points out a behavior that they "didn't do" only to find out later that they did actually do it, but were consciously unaware of the behaviors in question? This is a common occurrence.

Try this experiment just to prove this point for yourself. The next time you are in a face-to-face conversation with another person, mention the words "dry" and "lips" in your conversation, separately or together, but not in direct relation to the person you are speaking to and watch them lick their lips. They may continue to do this throughout the remainder of the interaction. They may even begin to bite the skin from their lips. What you have done is planted the idea of "dry lips" into their mind and it has now taken over their behaviors, albeit subtly. I wouldn't be surprised if you just licked your lips as you read this...suggestions can be that powerful.

As part of our goal of making "good men better," we are definitely referring to their behavior, psychology, and their beliefs; these are the three points of transformation mentioned earlier. If the reader gets nothing else from this chapter, I pray you to understand that we have a most efficient and effective means of acquiring this understanding. It is through the use of our culturally relevant rituals and rites, and a shifting of our worldview from the limited Western orientation, to one that incorporates views consistent with our African Ancestry, in tandem with that of the West. This will grant us an holistically superior perception of reality.

I will use the rest of this chapter to share portions of the blue print for a set of degrees that I have fully developed, which

An African Rite Considered

together make up an "African Rites" of Prince Hall Freemasonry. This is a proposed set of degrees, all based on true African spiritual mythologies and cultural traditions, featuring African-based symbolism and iconography. Like the other auxiliary Rites, the proposed African Rite will also follow the successful completion of the Blue degrees; in other words, it would only be available to Regular Master Masons. It is my hope, in presenting these degrees, that Brothers will give earnest consideration to the concepts and their related implications for our Craft. My qualifications for formulating this proposal include the fact that I have actually been initiated into several authentic African spiritual traditions and am qualified in these systems to perform specific rites for others.

African Rite – A Brief Outline of The Degrees

After completing the three degrees of the Blue Lodge, a well-qualified Brother is welcome to pursue further Light by way of the African Rite. Starting with the 4th Degree, this Rite is designed to take the candidate deeper into self-knowledge and self-mastery, by way of an initiation into

African ritual and symbolism. The rites are based on established African ritual and spiritual science, and are guided by the cosmological principles embedded in the Kemetic Puat Neteru as outlined by the "Tree of Life," and elaborated and detailed within the various versions of the Per-t Em Heru, as illustrated by the Pataki and Odu Ifa found in the Yoruba spiritual traditions, and various other African spiritual sciences.

This "house" expands upon the notion that Freemasonry continues to be a living vessel for the transmission of universal sacred wisdom, and the African mysteries are the teachings with the highest resonance for descendants of both Africa and the African Lodge. It is perhaps the missing link in our continued journey in search of the L___ W___. Gaining access to Freemasonry by successfully completing the three degrees of the Blue Lodge, the Master Mason has demonstrated his desire for more Light, and has taken the necessary steps to unlock the doors leading to the same.

In further pursuit of this Light, we have thus far followed the traditions that were created for and handed down by others. What good is the gaining of more Light if we don't in fact, become enlightened, self-sufficient, self-determining, and self-empowered by creating systems and processes that work for us, in ways that are determined by us, as guided by our Ancestral wisdom? When H.A. was found and raised to the "l_____g p_____r," his memories of who he was prior to the death blow were never restored, thereby leaving him incomplete, but functioning. He was left to the mercy of those who raised him, his trusted Brothers. If we see ourselves as H.A., and the following degrees as the restoration of our pre-trauma selves, we may become whole and our levels of functioning increased.

LODGE OF KHEPERA-U

4th Degree – Master of the Earthen Temple (Ptah – Creation Story, the Fashioner of Man; The Fashioners of Clay)

In this degree, the candidate is taken through the necessary procedures to realize a certain level of control over their physical vehicle. In addition to demonstrating mastery, the candidate must also have an active and observable commitment to improving at least one aspect of their physical health (based on what is identified to be underlying issues). According to the Egyptian creation story, Ptah sat at his potter's wheel fashioning Man from clay. The Neteru or heavenly beings that were responsible for this individual then breathed life into the clay, animating it and giving it purpose. Embedded in this story are certain principles that, once understood at the deepest levels, the candidate becomes more knowledgeable about all physical creation. The candidate represents Ptah in this degree.

<u>Knowledge, Skills, and Competencies to be developed</u>

- Knowledge of human anatomy and physiology specifically dealing with the interplay of the various body systems and how imbalances and health manifest on the physical, mental, and spiritual levels.

- Knowledge of how each and every human is a creator in and of themselves. Candidates will be provided with very specific examples and experiences to demonstrate how they are in fact a creative force.

- Knowledge of the Breath and the subtle energies of the Body

- Develop the skill to manipulate various body functions at will.

- Develop the skill to produce an original product from an original idea.

- Develop the skill of proper breathing in its various forms in order to experience the various functions and benefits.

- Competencies developed at this level include the ability to improve our current rough ashlars, eventually shaping them into the perfect ashlar. This will require us to correct at least one physical ailment with which we are currently dealing.

5th Degree – Expedition of Nun
(Auset – Journey in Search of Ausar)

The fifth degree involves the Traveler exploring and seeking to better understand their emotional state. They will be given the necessary information and practical experiences designed to develop the use of emotions as servants and no longer as leaders. Throughout the Story of Ausar and Auset, we are provided with instances wherein Auset is engulfed by her emotional state as it relates to the assault launched against her family, her husband, and their empire. She demonstrates how one channels the energy of emotion from a destructive and often self-defeating direction, into a productive and empowering one. Heru undergoes a similar experience when he sought to avenge his Father's death by battling his wicked uncle Set. At times, the young Heru's emotions got the best of him, causing him to lose several battles. It was not until he sought the Wisdom of Tehuti, that he was capable of finally subduing Set, and reestablishing order in his Father's kingdom. The candidate plays the role of Auset and Heru during this degree.

Knowledge, Skills, and Competencies to be developed

- Recognition and identification of the various emotional states experienced.

- Recognition and identification of the triggers of these emotional states.

- Recognition and identification of the thoughts (verbal and visual) that accompany these emotional states.

- Recognition and identification of the behaviors that precede as well as those that follow the on-set of these emotional states.

- Mastery over the emotional states within one's self.

- Mastery over the emotional states within others.

6th Degree - Apua-t: Opening the Way (Anpu/Sebek/Ap-uat)

The sixth degree takes the Traveler to the gates of the outer Temple of Karnak. Here is where the candidate proves himself worthy of entrance into the deeper mysteries by demonstrating insightful intellect and the ability to face challenges without resorting to the Lesser aspects of his being. This requires the solving of progressively more difficult logic puzzles, the answering of riddles, and the ability to reason through various scenarios. The candidate takes on the persona of Anpu during this degree.

Knowledge, Skills, and Competencies to be developed

- The ability to discern truth from falsehood.

- The ability to efficiently solve problems using intellect and reasoning.

- The ability to successfully navigate "crossroad" situations.

- The ability to control one's verbal thinking and silence mental chatter.

- The ability to demonstrate keen executive cognitive functioning.

7th Degree – Lord of the Temple (Neb-t Het)

The Lord of the Temple is Life itself. The rites associated with this degree bring to the Sojourner a direct experience of their vitality and Life Force energy as the source of Life itself. Techniques for awakening and directing Ra is the catalyst for the experiences associated with this degree. The candidate portrays Nebt Het during this degree.

Knowledge, Skills, and Competencies to be Developed

- The ability to master and use one's imagination and visualization faculties.

- The ability to sublimate and direct the sexual energy (Life Force, Qi, Chi, Libido)

- The ability to create and maintain internal and external harmony.

- The ability to abstain from all life-force-draining, and health damaging activities, thoughts, and attitudes.

- The ability to decipher and elaborate on the meaning of nature-based symbols.

THE LODGE OF THE SOLAR EYE

8th Degree – Utchat Aakut of Ra (Heru's Battle with Set)

Becoming the Master of the Temple is set into stone at this degree. The candidates are taken through their final tests, the successful completion of which solidifies their status as members of the Lodge of the Solar Eye. Psychic gifts are strengthened and the candidate has shown and proven the advanced capabilities of human beings through demonstrating the power of their personal will, and ability to make clear and concise decisions. The candidate portrays Heru during this degree.

Knowledge, Skills, and Competencies to be developed

- Development of clairvoyant abilities.

- Resolute decision making.

- Circumspect in perspective.

- Develop the gift of Men Ab (Stable Heart).

9th Degree – The Double Horizon (Akheru)

An indistractable focus yields its own set of benefits in the form of spiritual talents and gifts. The processes of this degree generate an intensity designed to burn away any lingering remnants of the previous conditionings. It is a degree of purification and protection. Self-discipline, focus, and a steadfast disposition are significant keynotes of the work to be done during this degree. The candidate portrays Herukhuti during this degree.

Knowledge, Skills, and Competencies to be developed

- The ability to self-monitor with precision.

- The ability to manipulate physiological functions via the Will.

- Fasting from certain foods and substances for a set period of time.

- Develop the tool of telepathy.

10th Degree – Weighing of the Heart (Maat and the Four Sons of Heru)

The Brother who gains entry into this Chamber of the African Rite is awakened to the process of clearing the unconscious of any remaining negative judgment generated by the self or others, based on known and imagined transgressions. It is at this degree that the candidates heart is weighed against the feather of Truth. The *42 Declarations of Maat* guide the work of this degree. They will be used as both declarations and affirmations, in the morning and the evening respectively. The candidate portrays a recently deceased initiate traveling through the Duat, and appearing in the Halls of Judgment during this degree.

Knowledge, Skills, and Competencies to be developed

- Recognition of the interdependency of all things in existence.

- The ability to live Truth at every opportunity.

- Skillful use and deciphering of analogies.

- The ability to identify the four temperaments in living situations and things.

REALM OF THE AM DUAT

11th Degree – Djed in Djeddjedu (Seker-t)

Initiates earn access to spiritual formulas and rituals they can perform for the benefit of their external and material lives. The work at this degree is designed to provide access to certain tools and keys for the use of spiritual power and the latent abilities of the mind. The candidate at this degree portrays Seker-t.

Knowledge, Skills, and Competencies to be developed

- Steadfastness in the face of difficulty.

- The ability to sit still for extended periods of time.

- Engage in deep levels of mediation and deep thought (SBA).

- The proficient use of certain mantras and formulas.

Endnotes

1	A phrase used to identify the Fifteen Founders of African Lodge #1, the origins of all regular Prince Hall Affiliated Grand Lodges. They are: Prince Hall, Cyrus Jonbus, Bueston Slinger, Prince Rees, John Canton, Peter Freeman, Benjamin Tiber, Duff Buform, Thomas Sanderson, Prince Rayden, Cato Speain, Boston Smith, Peter Best, Fortin Howard and Richard Tilley.

2	See "Worldview Chart" of esteemed Industrial and Organization Psychologist Edwin J. Nichols

3	In this context, transformation has three dimensions: psychological (changes in understanding of the self), convictional (revision of belief systems), and behavioral (changes in lifestyle).

4	Ontology is the study of reality, the nature of being and how things come to be.

5	See Carl G. Jung's "Red Book" for an example of the psychological torment experienced by the esteemed psychiatrist.

6	See any work by Mantak Chia for detailed explanations and practices related to the cultivation and intentional use of the life-force via sexual contact and intimacy.

The Masonic Mind Defined

Jeffery Menzise, Ph.D., 32°, FPS

*T*he mind. Where does it exist in your being? How does it function, and what is its purpose? Can it be manipulated? These are all questions that have been considered by humans for millenia. Even today, with all of our advanced technologies, we are hard pressed for a definition of "mind" that goes beyond the theoretical. Those in need of "concrete evidence" to decide the existence of a thing, will have a difficult time trying to satisfy this desire in regards to the governor of our mental activities and functions. Behavioral and biological psychologists tend to ascribe all aspects of the mind, including its genesis, to the physical brain. Perhaps the most fascinating of all organs, the brain and the nervous system seem to be a relay station of sorts, a switchboard, or control room from which we are able to interact with, and manipulate physical reality beginning with our own body.

Being made in the image of our Creator means that we have similar characteristics and qualities as the Creator. This is analogous to how a drop of water has the same basic molecular and atomic make up as the billions of water molecules forming a tidal wave. Not to minimize the immense difference between a drop of water and a tidal wave, but consider how one can quench thirst while the other may easily drown. Regardless of how it is moved to action, water is water; whether in your body or held captive in a cloud. Meaning, if the Creator is capable of creating, so are we. The evidence is the fact that we are here now...someone created us. Two brilliant "scientists" intuitively came together, mixed the appropriate substances (sex cells-gametes), delivered via perfected apparati (sex organs), and incubated in a perfected environment (the womb), and here we are; each one, the same basic way. This is true for all thoughts, ideas, inventions...everything.

Masonry, as our Brotherhood exists

today, has traveled far across the burning sands, journeyed through booby-trapped lands, and sought through the rubbish piles of former temples, only to have our quest for Light renewed with each circle around the square. Every now and then we come back with a jewel, a precious keystone, or knighted into the Royal Secret. All of these advancements are mere manifestations of a possibility within the mind and soul of the Brother traveling this path. Just as neurosurgeons are able to point to very specific parts of the physical brain and relate it to a mental function, we too should be capable of pointing to the specific parts of our Masonic ritual that are responsible for producing specific changes in our character and cognitive abilities, our person and our mentality. This, my Brothers, is the *Light* we have all been in search of.

    Our minds have, as its strength and weakness, the fact that they are highly sensitive and most impressionable. This curse-gift brings about the process by which we are able to grow and develop our Masonic Mind. By intentionally feeding your mind with things in line with your intended experience and outcome, one is capable of becoming the Supreme Will in their own life, second only to that which created minds; i.e., the Master of the Lodge.

Similar to the way we naturally and instinctively knew how to eat as children[1], our minds, too, have a reflex that allows us to assimilate information and other forms of energetic stimulation (sight, sound, smell, taste, touch, Light). Just as with a child, if we do not monitor closely what is being ingested, we may end up thwarting our own development, and perhaps retarding our growth.

The most important part of most journeys is the preparation that occurs before the first step is ever taken. In regards to the development of our Masonic Minds, this preparation consists of our early belief systems, personal biases, and the depth of our understanding of reality. As in the EA

---

1   The Rooting Reflex naturally makes a newborn attempt to ingest whatever is close to their mouths, the taste buds and nose positioned right above the mouth help with discerning between what is healthy and what is not.

degree, we begin with our compasses being limited and held within a certain range by the square that rests above it at 90°. This demonstrates, for the astute Craftsman, that although the potential exists for the drawing of a circle with a large diameter, the radius is purposely limited by our hoodwinked experiences, and thus, the circle will ALWAYS be within the square.

In our FC degree, one arm of the compass is freed up and allowed to move more freely, however, it remains limited by its complement remaining beneath the square; thus the circle will always overlap the square. This is similar to life, in that, we are often ill-prepared by our intellectual training, to truly use our spiritual gifts to its fullest potential, being hindered by our dependency and focus on our physical nature. This limitation is what causes preachers to backslide by committing the "sins" that they preach against, and is also what causes the medical doctor working at the "Cancer Center" to take several smoke breaks throughout their shift. It also allows Man to succumb to fears, and perform less than optimally due to being overcome by emotions.

In our Most Sublime Degree, that of a MM, we are raised from the dead to a living perpendicular "on the square," while our compasses are finally and simultaneously raised above the square. This "death" and "resurrection," although draped in allegory, is truly a scientific equation giving us the formula for freeing our True and Highest selves from the limitations of the physical; a process that allows us to encircle the square with a completed $360°^2$. Because we are pre-wired to access this feature of our being, we simply need to be pointed in the right direction and shown the location of this particular "light switch." Unfortunately, many of us discontinue our active quest for Light, even if we do gain access into the other "houses," and find ourselves "busy"

---

2   Isn't it interesting that the main symbols of our craft—the compass and square—are both used to draw geometric figures that both ALWAYS consist of 360° (a circle and square respectively), yet we only aspire for 33°...this very interesting observation is hidden in plain sight, yet many of us have NEVER noticed. Although we are practicing Symbolic Masonry, we would do well to learn the function of the symbols and tools as they are used in the Operative aspects of the Craft.

and therefore, we rarely return to our foundation of the Blue Lodge, in order to truly decipher the jewels that we left at the site of the temple ruins[3].

The "true" Masonic Mind is insatiable when it comes to seeking Light. It is forever on a quest to know more and to better understand all that comes into its sphere of awareness. The Masonic Mind seeks to uncover all the hidden aspects of its own nature for the purpose of character refinement, from the inside out. The Masonic Mind, in all of its mystery, is a beacon for attracting the pleasure and benefit of living a favored life; it draws to its possessor and

---

3   Some argue that this is the importance of the Red House (The Holy Royal Arch)—as the third section of the third degree—wherein the temple is completed and we find the Keystone, collect our wages, and receive the "True Word." Until this occurs, we are still Fellow Crafts, unable to be regularly compensated for our work. In fact, if one attempts to receive the wages prior to being "exalted," they will be treated as an imposter. There is truly something to the 3 X 3 X 3 and the "living arch" that our Companions should explore further...

cultivator, a sort of magic that others will notice and whisper about.

This magic will lead to a deeper power as long as the diameter of our circle continues to expand outwardly into the deepest recesses of creation. Should we become satisfied with the small gains, we will never realize that they are but drops in the bucket, and are laughable to one who knows how far it can really go. This is the very magic used by Solomon when he summoned the Angels to assist in the building of his temple; this is the very magic taught to Moses as he was being raised as an Egyptian priest and prince; the same magic that he used to free up his people suffering under the illegitimate reign of the foreign Pharoah.

How do we acquire and expand upon this Masonic Mind? The answer is in our symbolism. We would benefit greatly by observing the rule of our 24-inch gauge. By dividing our day into these three equal parts, and fully observing and understanding each aspect, we will likely become a more refined vehicle (as individuals as well as a collective organization).

The Masonic Mind Defined

For example, the 8-hours used in service to God and/or a distressed and worthy Brother, are the 8-hours within which we are to focus on our spiritual work and cultivation. This may take on many forms, however, it is strongly recommended that our service to God go beyond the weekly worship service and that it include intentional spiritual training designed to increase spiritual efficiency and awareness. In regards to serving a distressed Brother, what better way to assist than to show the way towards self-enhancement and self-improvement via the service to God (spiritual training to increase efficiency and awareness).

The 8-hours devoted to our usual vocation, from an enlightened perspective, becomes the testing grounds for us to prove our spiritual work. Oft times, we find ourselves in work situations that are stressful, unfulfilling, and perhaps totally lacking in the necessary and fair compensation necessary in order to live comfortably. If one is indeed doing the work outlined above as the first 8-hours, then this situation easily changes. The well-trained Masonic Mind is very clear that life is easily manipulated and changed through the use of basic techniques. Sometimes all that is needed is a shift in perspective, at other times, one may need to find an exit.

The last 8-hours, reserved for refreshment and sleep, is equally as powerful a tool as the others. In modern times, the notion of refreshment has been over-simplified and relegated to the task of taking in beverage and relaxing from the daily work. The Masonic Mind will immediately see the flaw in this interpretation and use of this time by simply analyzing the word "re-FRESH-ment." The prefix "re-" implies going back to a particular state, the root word "fresh" identifies the newness and reinvigorated state being sought, and the last syllable, "ment," could perhaps be referring to our mentality, or state of mind (the sleep aspect of these 8-hours deals with the renewal of the body as well). The importance of refreshment, from the perspective of an awakened Masonic Mind, is what allows us to utilize sleep in its most effective manner. There is a process by which enlightened individuals utilize their sleep-time to accomplish important tasks, solve difficult problems, and learn new information and techniques.

  Sometimes called Lucid Dreaming, this process is what allows the "sleeper" to maintain their conscious awareness from the waking-state into the dream-state. Simply stated, the individual is aware of the moment that they "go to sleep,"[4] and thus, maintain a level of awareness that they are dreaming while the dream is taking place. This allows for a person to not only function in a dream as they do in their daily lives, but also allows one to determine their dreams and to utilize this very powerful state of consciousness as a laboratory for training and improving their propensities to function in the waking state. Think about it, many of us only realize we were asleep once we wake up; and many of us only realize we were dreaming when the dream has finished. Imagine being able to walk right up

---

4 Note the difference here between "falling asleep" and "going to sleep." The former deals with an unconscious slipping into sleep, while the latter refers to the intentional directing of the waking state into the sleep state.

to the door of "sleep," insert your key, gain entry and consciously live-out the dream *while* dreaming. The scared individual having a nightmare would now be able to consciously confront the fear and neutralize the threat.

The person who goes to sleep anxious about a very important meeting, is now equipped to conduct the meeting in their dream state, affording the opportunity to rehearse, prepare, and gain insight. As you can see, this ability to maintain consciousness (awareness) across several states of consciousness (awakeness) is one of the most valuable lessons found at the core of many ancient systems of initiation and spiritual cultivation[5]. It would benefit us greatly to become knowledgeable of both the philosophy and practical application.

Overall, it is important for us Travelers to understand that we are fully capable of going above and beyond the self-imposed limitations given to us through our socialization and environmentally imposed boundaries. We as Freemasons have been equipped with every tool necessary to not only think outside of the box, but to also function outside of the box. It's that mysterious form of knowing that attracted many of us to the Craft in the first place. Now that we have been "raised," it is our duty and responsibility to develop and cultivate our Masonic Minds.

Freemasonry and the African Influence

Jeff Menzise, Ph.D., 32°, FPS

(Interviewed by PM Alton G. Roundtree, 33°)

First, give us a synopsis of your learning and experiences that make you a sound source on the subject.

I am an initiate of several African Spiritual Traditions, each of which contains its very own "Mystery System." I was initiated into two of them prior to becoming a Freemason, and the third after being admitted into the Consistory and joining the Council of Royal and Select Masters. This unique opportunity afforded me the ability to observe Freemasonry as an Initiated Priest of African spirituality, and also the ability to experience African spiritual initiation via the lens of Freemasonry. What I can say, beyond the shadow of any doubt, is that these are all systems based on the exact same and precise spiritual science, all of which can be found within the immortal records of the Nile Valley, and the many other ancient African civilizations.

In addition to my personal experience as an initiate of several African spiritual traditions and sciences, I am also a doctor of clinical psychology. This professional and academic training has provided me various tools for understanding human development, developmental processes, the human mind, soul, capabilities, etc., all of which are the main subjects of Freemasonry, and all other systems of initiation. I am a skilled clinician, and a master symbolist. My symbol interpretation skills were developed during both my clinical and spiritual training. Clinically, the substance of the unconscious mind is thought to be coded in deep symbolism, therefore, any effective analyst will need to know how to interpret dreams, body language (including facial expression), patterns and content of speech, as well as many other expressions of the subconscious mind. This lens allows me to look at our Masonic symbols within the context of a system of symbols, emerging from the unconscious minds of Man, from immemorable times.

Bringing the subconscious and unconscious to the level of conscious awareness, is one of the early steps an initiate must take when seeking enLIGHTenMENT; it is also the main purpose of psychoanalytic therapy (a system developed by Sigmund Freud and later expanded by Carl Jung, both of whom studied ancient African wisdom traditions). My experience as a clinical psychologist has also given me many opportunities to witness true human transformation, via the employment of specifically designed protocols (rituals), with consistent and reliable outcomes. Knowing and having experienced these transformative processes both first and second hand, I do not have to speculate on the reality of the sentiments portrayed by Freemasonry and other Mystery Schools. I have both gone through them, and have facilitated the initiation processes of others. I am both blessed and fortunate to have had these experiences and to have gained the insight afforded by such a configuration of spiritual tools and life experiences.

Who, in your opinion, are the credible writers that emphasize African culture and the contributions of Africans in the development of freemasonry in Europe?

There are many credible writers that emphasize African culture and the contributions of Africans in the development of Freemasonry in Europe. We have: Dr. Asa Hilliard, Dr. Yosef ben Jochannan, Anthony Browder, Professor James Smalls, George G.M. James, Ra Un Nefer Amen, Wayne Chandler, Theophile Obenga, Dr. T.M. Stewart, R.A. Schwaller de Lubicz, Isha Schwaller de Lubicz, Peter Thompkins, Laird Scranton, Robert Buvall, J. Anthony West, Gerald Massey, Maspero, Grote, Madame Blavatsky, Norman Frederick de Clifford, M.W. Blackden, M.A. Atwood, W.L. Wilmhurst, Isabel Cooper-Oakley, and of course I must include myself in this ever-growing list.

What is the position of the writers you mentioned and do you agree with them?

Many of the writers mentioned above demonstrate how the Ancient Wisdom traditions of African societies migrated into Europe via the education received by early Greeks and Romans in the Nile Valley.

Some demonstrate how both Pythagoras and Euclid received education and training in the Nile Valley, and how that training led them to evolve as humans, granting them greater understanding and enlightenment as regards the universe and its laws. Each of them present facts and perspectives to varying degrees; some focusing solely on the historical data of dates and names of individuals and their interactions, while others delve deeper into the content of the so-called "Mystery Schools," and how they were designed to evolve humans beyond their mere physical consciousness. Regardless of which of these two groups the author belongs, there is a relatively common thread that runs throughout their perspectives regarding the relationship between African spirituality and Freemasonry.

This thread typically presents modern initiation rites, including Freemasonry, to be a direct attempt at imitating, and/or the unbroken continuation of, the so-called "Mystery Schools" found amongst ancient Africans. This continuation and/or imitation focused on the transfiguration of the quality of one's Soul, and the ability to present this quality consistently and on demand. The degree to which an individual is capable of demonstrating their true spiritual and divine nature, is directly related to their degree of initiation. To quote Hermes, as mentioned by Stewart, "the Aeonic Consciousness is gained by 'purging out of the tendencies of the lower nature and replacing them by the energies of the Divine Powers. It is the will of man alone that can turn the powers of the Soul 'downwards' or 'upwards.' This is the exact sentiment conveyed by the Masonic creed to 'square our actions by the square of virtue with all mankind...' and to 'circumscribe our desires and keep our passions within due bounds.' It should be clear at this point that there is an intentional coincidence relating the 'Star of David' ('Seal of Solomon') to the Masonic Compass and Square."

In my book, Symbolically Speaking, I detail the correlations between Ancient African spiritual traditions/initiations and the modern versions of the Masonic Craft, as both an initiate of several African Spiritual traditions tracing their lineage back to Ancient Wisdom and processes, and as a 32° Freemason, descending from African Lodge #1.

How has Egyptian Mysticism impacted modern mainstream thought?

For the purpose of this interview, I shall intentionally take a different approach to answering this question. I am doing this to assist our general readership, and the Craft specifically, to view the breadth and depth of Egyptian Mysticism as a very powerful tool that can be utilized in various ways; similar to how a screwdriver can be used to build a house, and also as a lethal weapon, in the hands of the same person. In this light, I see that Egyptian Mysticism has impacted and influenced modern mainstream thought in various, but subtle ways.

From my perspective, mainstream thinking, meaning the thinking of the masses, is not necessarily in-line with Egyptian Mysticism, but is being manipulated by those whose thinking IS in-line with Egyptian Mysticism. In other words, those that influence the thinking of the masses are typically using principles and processes that are in line with Egyptian Mysticism. For example, Hitler's Minister of Propoganda, Joseph Goebbles, and the equally powerful propagandist Edward L. Bernays (who was the nephew of Sigmund Freud), both carried on in much the same tradition by seeking to understand the deeper mysteries of the human mind and soul.

Both Bernays' and Goebbles' jobs were to understand human nature in order to manipulate and master people. Goebbles' marketing campaign shaped the mind of an entire nation, leading it on a deadly campaign towards global domination. While Bernays employed the same tools, except to manipulate consumer habits, and to amass a fortune via capitalistic marketing. They both achieved their goals through the use of images, slogans, body language, and emotional coercion.

If modern mainstream thought aligned more with Egyptian Mysticism, there'd be an entirely different caliber of people in society; a people who were less susceptible to the propaganda-based tactics of Goebbles and modern mass media. This caliber of people would reflect what Hermes calls the "Aeonic Consciousness," what R. A. Schwaller de Lubicz calls "the Pharonic Mind," and what is referred to by Ra Un Nefer Amen as an "Ausarian."

Each of these labels describes a person who has squared their behaviors and who have circumscribed their passions. This is done, in part, by adhering to the principles of Maat while raising one's consciousness beyond the base realities of the physical and emotional states, to those of the spiritual and higher-mind-consciousness states. How one identifies also plays a major part in this quest towards the "living p_____r."

If, for example, an individual identifies predominantly with their physical selves, complete with the limitations and gifts associated therewith, they will be less likely to harness and cultivate the latent powers of the mind and soul. This is the effect of living in poverty, hungry, sickly, or in torturous situations, or engulfed in physical pleasures...it focuses one's attention, and therefore their energy (life force), towards the physical. However, if one has identified as a triune being, meaning one with three aspects: mind, body, and soul/spirit, they are likely to seek to develop all three levels to one degree or another, providing for more tools and an expanded opportunity to function masterfully in the world.

In modern times, we have a few who have mastered the principles of Egyptian Mysticism, some of which are using this knowledge to maintain control over the masses, and to reap massive benefits for themselves. While other enlightened individuals remain ever watchful for the slightest stirring in their Brethren, indicating their dissatisfaction with their current state of existing, and a glimmer in their soul, signifying their yearning to be more than what they perceive themselves to be.

This latter group, of which modern day PHA Freemasonry is predominately populated by, have taken the first step to become the "Mortals," and then eventually the "Intelligences," and ultimately the "Sons of Light." The fact that every Brother in the Craft has entered into this process on their own free will and accord, while also professing their belief in the immortality of the soul, have symbolically placed themselves in a group of individuals who are now qualified to advance in their spiritual quest.

      This is not an automatic progression. In fact, in order to advance through these three degrees of Egyptian Initiation, a Brother has to be willing to raise both points of the c_____s above the s_____e; meaning, they must be willing to refine themselves, in every aspect, shedding away conditionings and those attributes that limit their ability to realize their full potential. We are presented with this notion at every single degree within the masonic body, however, we are never actually and intentionally engaged in a process that allows us to actually undergo this transformative process that will awaken the gifts associated with each degree; except of course the training of our memories while doing our "D_____e W__k."

      In the 2017 volume of the Lux e Tenebris transcripts, I proposed an "African Rite" to facilitate such a process. This African Rite consists of degrees developed to engage the initiate in practical degree work, which will train their minds and souls to consciously seek the levels of refinement mentioned earlier. This is done through the lens of an African-centered worldview, based on an African-centered set of mythologies.

It is understood that the culture and symbolism utilized by our modern version of the Craft is beneficial, but not optimally so. It has been well documented that cultural relevancy plays a major role in the effectiveness of any tool, be it educational, psychological or spiritual. It is from this understanding that I have designed the degrees of the African Rite, and from my experience as a clinical psychologist, an African Initiate, and Freemason, that I have developed this process to include elements proven to awaken these faculties that lie dormant within each of us. This opportunity is available to those who are willing to put forth the effort and sacrifice required to advance to the higher levels of their own humanness.

How did Masonic traditions evolve out of Egyptian Mysticism?

There are a few lines connecting Egyptian Mysticism to modern Masonic traditions. One is via the teachings of Pythagoras and Euclid, and even the central roles played by Hiram Abiff and King Solomon, both of whom are stated to have lived in what could easily be considered a part of the Egyptian cultural reach during ancient times (both Tyre and Solomon's empire were just a short distance across the Mediterranean Sea from Egypt; with Solomon actually marrying an identifiably African wife).

The other route is through the research of Ancient African philosophy, conducted by early explorers and historians, and the founders of the predecessors to modern freemasonry. These secret societies of yesteryear have worked to maintain their knowledge, wisdom, and understanding, and have worked to transmit this information to future generations.

To quote Grote,

> The allegorical interpretation of myths has been by several learned investigators, especially Cruezer, connected with the hypothesis of an ancient and highly instructed body of priests, having their origins in either Egypt or in the East, and communicated to the rude and barbarous Greeks, religion, physical, and historical knowledge, under the veil of symbols.
> - Every Man's Library Edition of Grote, vol. 2, p. 81

Many ancient and highly respected Greek and Roman philosophers either directly or indirectly paid homage to the teachings derived from Egypt, that assisted with the civilizing of Greece and its subsidiary nations. These philosophers include, but are not limited to the following: Iamblichus, Socrates, Plato, Proclus, Hippocrates, Herodotus, Orpheus, and Appolonius. Homage to Egypt, in regards to her role in the spread of divinely-based wisdom, is also found cloaked in the Holy Bible of modern Christians. This can be found in the story of the *Exodus*. Within this story, we find that Moses is raised in the Mysteries of the Ancient Egyptian priesthood, and is actually raised as a Prince. He distributes these teachings amongst his followers who are thought to be the ancestors of the modern-day Jew, of which, King Solomon was an initiated priest, a master Mason, and a King.

      King Solomon's intimate dealings with the African "Queen of Sheba," Makeda, as detailed in the Kebra Negast, is a metaphor demonstrating how the mingling of foreign nations with those of Africa, has produced beneficial progeny for the former, who have returned to Africa to restore her greatness (this is the story of Menelik, son of Solomon and Makeda, and his return of the Ark of the Covenant to his mother's land of Ethiopia. It is said to currently be housed at the "Church of Our Lady Mary of Zion" in Axum, Ethiopia). As a side-note, some also believe the story of Exodus to be a tale of indigenous Africans fleeing Egypt to escape the rule of foreign invaders, taking with them the mysteries of Egypt to start their civilizations elsewhere, including Israel amongst the Israelites.

Does freemasonry benefit from the study and understanding of Egyptian mysticism?

Freemasonry, and therefore freemasons, ABSOLUTELY benefit from the study of Egyptian Mysticism. It is through this study that I was fully capable of seeing the mysteries "hidden in plain sight" within our Masonic ritual. The study of Egyptian Mysticism has the potential to open the minds of modern Freemasons to include the possibilities that what we claim to know about reality is far more limited than reality itself. With this understanding, we will begin to see the symbolism left for us to interpret and apply within our Masonic rituals. The study should not only be intellectual, it should also be practical. The practical aspect of Egyptian Mysticism deals directly with the cultivation of human capabilities above and beyond those commonly thought to be the limitations of modern man. The conscious cultivation of the mind, body, and soul is what we hear throughout our various degrees, however, we rarely get an opportunity to systematically achieve these goals through our travels.

    As previously mentioned, the proposed African Rite, consisting of degrees designed to facilitate this practical growth and development, is the next logical step in our continued recovery from what we know to be the "d____h b___w" delivered by the R_____n with a s_____g m___l. Looking at this allegory, from both a literal and figurative perspective, we can find an abundance of jewels. One very important discovery I have made on my own journey is the relationship between a traumatic brain injury, amnesia, and the need to restore pre-trauma memories "lost" (retrograde amnesia) as a result of the attack.

    In the story of Hiram Abiff, his pre-trauma memory is never restored after he is raised. We only see him being raised by one of the other Grand Masters present, leaving us to understand that he went forward in the way of that particular Master; never returning to the culture that initially raised him, and through which he achieved his degrees. This is important because we can still see ourselves functioning in this manner, meaning we continue in the way of those who "raised" us, after we have awakened from the death-blow of Enslavement and colonization. Because it is a master who raised us, we are capable of functioning, albeit not to our fullest potential, and not independent of the ones who have conducted the initial "resurrection."

      Remember it took several attempts to get "us" back "upright." This is an important point to consider especially when speaking of the influence of, or the relationship between, the Egyptian Mysteries and how it may benefit us to study them. Again, in this context, the study of the Egyptian Mysteries will serve the purpose of reclaiming our "pre-death blow" states of consciousness and beingness; thereby restoring our independence, and abilities to build more bountiful temples and societies for ourselves. As evidence of spiritually-deficient state, I often cite the disparities found between PHA Grand Lodges, and those of "mainstream" Freemasonry. They are clearly utilizing the Craft in ways that yield different results than the manner in which we have been taught to use it.

    The proposed African Rite is based on my knowledge and experiences as an initiate and priest of various African spiritual traditions, and draws heavily from my experience as a doctor of clinical psychology. The awakening of latent talents and skills within the modern Mason, is what will truly set our Craft, specifically as descendants of the African Lodge, on a trajectory that ensures success, prosperity, and longevity. Hence, the need for an understanding of Ancient Egyptian mysticism.

What are the major tenants of Egyptian mysticism?

The main tenant of Egyptian Mysticism is that man is a divine being and that there are specific pathways to actualizing this divinity. The science of nature is used to facilitate the process of growing beyond our imposed limitations, and emerging fully into our true selves, complete with methods for walking as powerful creators of our own destiny, with dominion over all things. The process by which Egyptian Mysticism achieves these goals and states of being, is sometimes diametrically opposed to our modern way of approaching knowledge and power. It is the reason for us being required to "die" to the world, in order to be "reborn" more powerful, efficient, and effective as humans. Bergsen says it in the following way:

> We recognize the unity of spiritual life only when we place ourselves in intuition, in order to go from intuition to

intellect, for from intellect, we shall never pass into intuition.

He is telling us that the modern, and popular means of approaching life, the intellectual, is incapable of leading us to the more beneficial intuitive method. He continues by letting us know that the intuitive is also the superior method for approaching the intellectual because an intuitive person is also fully capable of embracing intellect and information; while a purely intellectually-dependent person is limited in their ability to utilize their intuition to discern further information, and to develop a deeper understanding of the same.

According to some Masonic historians, freemasonry is based on the principles and values of ancient Egypt. Do you agree with this position?

I absolutely agree with this position. The principles and values of Ancient Egypt are based on universal knowledge and principles. It is important to understand this fact for several reasons. First, universal knowledge and principles are found universally; meaning they are the same regardless of space and time. With this understanding, it becomes clear that the "universal principles" found in modern freemasonry are the EXACT SAME universal principles and truths found in Ancient Egypt.

Second, we must also understand that something being based on the same principles, does not mean that they are implemented and manifested in the same way. The values of modern freemasonry, as written in the ritual, and in the interpretation of the many symbols, reflect the same principles as laid out in Ancient Egypt, specifically those ideals that relate to the immortality of the soul, and man's quest to actualize his highest, divine characteristics through the working of his Craft. The acknowledgment of the human body as the ultimate temple of the GAOTU (Grand Architect of the Universe), is encoded in both the principles of Ancient Egypt, as well as the principles of modern freemasonry.

Third, understanding this notion will allow us to also see that Ancient wisdom and principles, applied through various individuals, cultures, races, and organizations, will often manifest different and receive various degrees of proficiency when being applied practically. This is illustrated by the following analogy: Two people, a teenager that just received his driver's license and a NASCAR racing professional, both have an opportunity to drive a brand new Mustang 5.0. Each has access to the same vehicle, with no modifications, however, when the rubber meets the road, the NASCAR racer is capable of bringing forward certain characteristics of the Mustang that the teenager has no clue even exist.

On the surface, without knowing the differences in the drivers, an observer might assume that the vehicles are somehow different, and that this accounts for the variation in how the car drives. In reality, the vehicle (principle) is exactly the same, the difference in performance is due to the development and expertise of the drivers. It is the same when speaking about how modern organizations, such as freemasonry, manifest the principles and values of Ancient Egyptian wisdom. In many cases, the principles aren't readily recognizable to the common observer, but are there at its core nonetheless.

What Role Does The Book of the Dead (The Book of Coming Forth by Day) Play in the Connection of Egyptian Mysticism to Freemasonry?

If you study the Per-t Em Heru, you will recognize it as a book detailing not only the soul's travel through the "underworld" (Duat), but also as a manual for living to ensure that you are functioning optimally while here amongst the living. It is an initiation manual that has evaded comprehension by the majority of so-called Egyptologists. To grasp this concept, one must view the text and its myriad of symbols, from the worldview of an African. This holistic perspective will help to peel away the veils that impede our ability to accept the truth about our nature. You will find in the Per-t Em Heru a progression of an initiate through various degrees (gates), advancing closer and closer to their goal of becoming an Ausar (enLIGHTened person). You will find certain "Tylers" guarding the various gates, to whom the initiate must convey the correct passwords in order to gain entrance into the next phase of their journey.

    Viewing our various degrees and rituals as the multitude of gates featured in the Per-t Em Heru, you will find the layout and basic blueprints to be the same. The major difference is that the Ancients actually put these degrees into practice, and enjoyed a true "Coming Into the Light," which came as a natural result of performing the rituals therein described.

What Are Your Thoughts on Ancient Egyptian Hieroglyphs and Masonic Emblems (Level, Square, Compasses, etc.)?

There are some symbols found in Ancient Egyptian writings that are similar to the masonic working tools that we find in our modern Craft. There are also found operative masonic working tools used by the Master Craftsmen of Ancient times.

These symbols and tools are very consistent and both relate to the building of temples. There is no question in my mind that these symbols and tools were borrowed from ancient civilizations by our modern craft. It is more than a mere coincidence because the tools were used in the exact same way in modern building as they were in ancient times. The difference is the fact that the speculative aspect of these symbols, as we currently view them, is missing the practical application enjoyed in ancient times. The fact that modern builders still don't understand how the ancient masters built their temples, serves as more evidence supporting this fact.

Would You Consider the Many Egyptian Theme Rooms that can be Found in Masonic Temples and Buildings as an Acknowledgment of the Influence of Ancient Egyptian Mysticism?

They absolutely are. The amount of resources poured into the creation of these rooms and buildings speaks to the importance of Egypt in the establishment of our modern craft. The Egyptian Room, found in the Grand Lodge of Pennsylvania, was the first to be constructed in the building, and, was designed to model a real Egyptian temple room. According to the brother who unlocked the room for me to analyze, they actually sent someone to Egypt in order to observe a true temple room in order to get the model correct.

The House of the Temple, in Washington, DC, boasts of being crowned by a step pyramid, while brandishing two stylized Sphinxes out front. In addition to these things, you will also find two statues of Egyptian priests in the main lobby and a Heru Bedhet on the wall.

According to my tour guide, these two statues have an interesting history. The stone was quarried from upstate New York, then shipped by train to Union Station in Washington, DC. Train tracks were specially laid between Union Station and 16th Street, NW, where the House of the Temple is located, in order to transport the stone, and then the tracks were taken up. Once the stones reached their destination, they were styled as two Egyptian initiates, complete with hieroglyphs carved onto their robes.

The amount of resources devoted to do these things speaks volumes of the importance that it must carry. There is also a tribute to the Kemetic Neter-t (Goddess) Auset hidden within the very architecture. The astute observer must be standing at a specific point in the main gallery, looking towards the cascading stairwell in order to see this symbol hidden in plain sight. It has consistently amazed me that our "mainstream"

Brothers so openly give praise and credit to our African Ancestors, while we in our PHA lodges seem to be hesitant or otherwise incapable of doing the same. Imagine how powerful our rituals and degree work would be, within the context of an African-styled Lodge.

    My intention is to bring this ideal to popularity within PHA, and eventually to manifest physically within our institution by way of Lodge décor and ritual practice.

What Do You Say About the Old Manuscripts Acknowledging the Influence of Egypt in the Development of Freemasonry?

    In some cases, Masonry is interchangeable with Geometry...a high level of which was found in the Nile Valley, where it is known to have been mastered by Man, earlier than anywhere else. The notion that it began with Euclid is a fallacy. Euclid is thought to have lived in around 300BCE. The pyramids, and various other temples in Kemet, predate his arrival and the reign of the Ptolemies by at least 3,000 years (according to some estimates). The geometry and craft masonry observable in Kemet are all evidence of this high science being ancient in Kemet long before any European was allowed to be initiated into Her mysteries.

These documents both mention Egypt specifically, and both include mention of the teachings of Greek scholars who are known to have been initiated into the mysteries of Ancient Egypt. Specific to these two documents, namely "The 15 Articles of Masons," as contained in the <u>Halliwell Manuscript</u> (Regis Poem), we find a mirroring of the moral and ethical code of Pharonic Egypt. This is consistent with Peter Thompkins' finding that King Athelstane utilized a unit of measurement in a way consistent with that of the Pharoahs of Kemet.

Specifically, there was land measured radiating from the King's abode, which was deemed holy/sacred; an area within which, if a crime was committed, it was taken as a direct offense to the crown.

Other ancient Lore finds the settling of Scotland by Scotia, who herself was Kemetic royalty...many of us are members of what is known as the Scottish Rite.

What Do You Say About the Following Comment?

> *"Masonic author, Albert Mackey, believed in a relationship between modern Freemasonry and Ancient Egypt. Wrote Mackey: 'The identity of design and method in the two systems, as illustrated by the division—into steps, classes, or degrees—to which both were subjected, viz., lustration (purification, or preparation), initiation, and perfection.'"*

> **(Gaia Staff, The Connection Between Ancient Egyptian Mystery Schools and Freemasonry, February 13, 2017)**

In short, I would say that Mackey's statements are very consistent with the way that others have drawn the connection between African Spirituality and Freemasonry. As stated earlier, the actual spiritual cultivation seems to be missing from our modern rendering of the Craft, and because of this, we are incapable of actualizing our full potential as Freemasons. People will try to use this perspective as evidence that the two "systems" are separate and only loosely related, sharing only a common "approach" or "blueprint." To me, this is similar to how a 1970s Plymouth Volare' shares the same basic blueprint as a 2018 Porsche or Jaguar. They end up being two totally different vehicles, in sophistication, form, and function. Having a blueprint that is basically the same is precisely what makes them one and the same thing, vehicles. There are more similarities than there are differences between the two vehicles, and the differences are oft times superficial, while the similarities are found at the core level.

      I would also caution our Brothers to not mistake our current inability to actualize the principles, for an absence of these principles.

Lastly, What Readings Would You Recommend For One Who Wants to Become Conversant on the Subject of Freemasonry and African Influences?

I recommend the following list for anyone interested in learning more about the spiritual aspects of African philosophy and modern freemasonry. It is important for those seeking to understand the relationship between modern freemasonry and Ancient African spiritual philosophy to be able to comprehend various aspects of African spiritual philosophies, African worldview, and some of the more historical and so-called "speculative" and "operative" understandings of these ancient systems.

It is my understanding that without this background, it will be virtually impossible to engage in a discussion regarding the relationship between these two, seemingly different, entities.

<u>Metu Neter vols. 1 & 2</u>
Ra Un Nefer Amen

Anybook by R. A. Schwaller de Lubicz and Isha Schwaller de Lubicz

<u>Bantu Philosophy</u>
Placid Temples

<u>Symbolism of the Gods of the Egyptians & the Light They Throw on Freemasonry</u>
T.M. Stewart

<u>Symbolically Speaking vol. 1</u>
Jeff Menzise

<u>Freemasonry of the Ancient Egyptians</u>
Manly P. Hall

<u>The Language of Secrecy: Symbols and Metaphors in Poro Ritual</u>
Beryl Bellman

<u>The Lost Keys of Freemasonry</u>
Manly P. Hall

Ritual of the Mystery of the Judgment of the Soul
M.W. Blackden

The House of the Hidden Places and The Book of the Master
W. Marsham Adams

Serpent in the Sky
J. Anthony West

Secret Practices of the Sufi Freemasons
Baron Rudolf von Sebottendorff

Mysteries of the Mind: Memphite Theology, The Philosophy of Ptah, and the Path to Immortality
Muata Ashby

Stellar Theology and Masonic Astronomy
Robert H. Brown

Symbolism of Mathematics and What Every Mason Should Know About Numbers
Milton A. Pottenger

Egyptian Mysteries: New Light on Ancient Spiritual Knowledge
Lucy Lamy

Ancient Operative Masonry and the Mysteries of Antiquity
S. R. Parchment

Kemet and the African Worldview
Maulana Karenga & Jacob Carruthers (eds.)

Egypt: Child of Africa
Ivan Van Sertima

Egypt Revisited
Ivan Van Sertima

Anything Written by Dr. Asa Hilliard

Other Mind on the Matter Publications

www.ingramcontent.com/pod-product-compliance
Lightning Source LLC
Chambersburg PA
CBHW040307170426
43194CB00022B/2926